PILGRIMAGE

Paul D. Newpower

**Paul David Newpower
1941–2023**

Family members, Maryknoll colleagues and classmates, and friends of Paul Newpower have produced and distributed this copy of Paul's 2009 memoir, *Pilgrimage*, to honor his memory and to give thanks for the many ways Paul enriched our lives.

© 2023. Family of Paul D. Newpower
All rights reserved.

ISBN: 9798374237306
Imprint: Independently published

Cover image: Unduavi Valley, Bolivia, 22 July 2009, photograph taken by Jimmy Harris

Pilgrimage was written in September 2009. Edited and published in January 2023 by Tom Fenton and Mary Heffron

Contents

Achacachi Siege 5
Achacachi 14
Dreams 15
Seminary. 19
Pastoral Experiences 24
Formation for Mission 31
Ordination for Bolivia 35
Bolivia and Latin America 39
La Paz, Bolivia 45
Colonel Banzer Takes Power 52
Liberation Theology 57
Achacachi Mission 59
Class Conflicts 63
Religious Conflicts 67
Cultural Conflicts 75
Loneliness 80
New Start 82
Formation of Aymará Leaders 83
Marriage Rites 87
Aymará Cosmology 90
Outsiders 97
Winding Down 101
Sojourn Back to the USA 107
Central America in Revolution 111
    Nicaragua 111
    El Salvador 113
    Guatemala and Honduras 114
Minneapolis 116

Maryknoll, New York 120
El Salvador Revisited 123
Films. 129
Achacachi Revisited 130
Companions 132
Archbishop Hélder Câmara 134
Spiritual Renewal 137
Cuba 139
Refugee Camp, Mexico 143
Bolivia Again. 145
USA Again. 147
Cochabamba. 150
Rebeca 154
Video Productions. 156
Wedding Bells 159
Getting a Job. 165
Family 168
Bolivian Politics 170
The Pilgrimage Continues 172

Appendix 1. *Interchange* Interview 174
Appendix 2. Obituary 179
Photo Credits 181

Achacachi Siege

TWO BOLIVIAN SOLDIERS were waiting for us at the entrance to town, with guns at ready. They stopped our vehicle and asked who we were. I was driving and told them we were the Maryknoll priests from this town. They said, "We were waiting for you."

They jumped on the running boards and told us to proceed into town. Everything was strangely quiet in the Aymará town of Achacachi, where I had been working for only a few months. All the doors to the houses were closed and no one was on the streets. I spotted our ambulance driver, Emilio, half hidden in a doorway, and called out to him to come over. He was obviously afraid, but approached us. I asked him what was happening. He said, "They attacked the convent."

My heart stopped. The convent! The Sisters had all gone with us to a meeting of religious leaders in the neighboring town of Compi. But they had left a group of young Aymará Indian girls in a study course. And then there were…the three students from the university hiding out. The new military government had found out about them on their witch-hunt of suspected opponents and came after them!

I turned off the main road and headed straight for the convent, against the protests of the two soldiers accompanying us. When we saw the convent, it was covered with bullet holes. All the windows had been shattered. A white flag was flying in one corner of the compound. An armed man stopped us at the entrance. I yelled at him, "What happened?" "We got the guerrillas!" he replied.

I pushed my way in, against his protests, shouting that I was the priest from this place and demanded to pass. Reluctantly, he let me and the other priests in our vehicle enter the convent. It was in shambles. The military had ripped apart everything looking for weapons, the furniture, cabinets, the ceiling, floor boards. Even the tabernacle, which holds the sacred Eucharist for Mass, had been smashed and emptied. The rest of the convent was empty of any other belongings, which I later learned the military had taken as "booty of war."

As we entered the kitchen, I noticed a big pool of blood on the floor and cried out, "What happened here?" fearing they had killed the woman who was the cook. The soldier proudly replied that they had killed one of the "guerrillas" there.

The armed guard told us we were under arrest and had to report to the local police station. I furiously drove there, wanting to confront the perpetrators of this atrocious attack. At the police station, they told us that the military had come out from La Paz to capture the three "guerrillas they knew were hiding out in the convent." They told us they killed one in a gunfight and captured the other man and woman.

I had known all three of them. The Sisters had introduced me to them several weeks earlier. They were three students from the San Andrés University in La Paz who had to escape from the city because of the repression of the new right-wing government of Colonel Hugo Banzer. He had come to power in a bloody coup that overthrew a left-wing government. Now he was on a rampage to round up suspected communists and all supporters of the previous government, imprison them, exile them or worse, torture them for information. Hundreds of people suffered such a fate, and many of them were killed.

The Sisters had introduced me to the three students a month before and explained that they were friends of theirs, had not committed any crimes, but because of their political views, were now being hunted down by the government. We knew that the government was raiding houses, even religious houses, in the city, looking for communist sympathizers. But I really did not believe they would come out to the rural areas looking for their victims. The three students had been studying medicine and were helping out at the dispensary in the convent. One of them even accompanied me out to some of the isolated mountain villages to care for the sick.

After taking power in a bloody coup in 1971 right-wing dictator Colonel Hugo Banzer went on a rampage rounding up suspected communists and all supporters of the previous government. Hundreds of Bolivians were imprisoned and tortured. Some were exiled.

House Arrest

After a brief interrogation at the police station, the military took us back to the parish house, where we were confined under house arrest. Actually, there were thirteen of us that had left that morning from different towns in the rural areas north of La Paz, known as the Altiplano. The group included the bishop, Briny Schierhoff, seven Sisters, and five priests.

At the parish house, we found our cook, Inés, in a state of shock, and all the girls from the convent course. At least they were all safe. Their parents had heard the shooting and had come into town for fear for their daughters. One of the young girls was Encarnación Huanca, about twenty years old and our best religious leader. She had been in charge of teaching the course in our absence.

She told us what had happened. Armed men burst into

her course at the convent and demanded to know where the "guerrillas" were. Encarnación boldly confronted them and said she didn't know anything about "guerrillas," and told them to leave them to teach their course. The armed men pushed their way through a door and into the clinic part of the convent. They started up the stairs to the second floor and were stopped by gunfire, which wounded the first intruder. The others retreated outside of the building. Apparently one of the students had a gun for protection, knowing that if they were captured by the military, they would be tortured or killed. He grabbed the machine gun from the wounded man and retreated back upstairs. Then the exchange of gunfire began.

The girls all escaped outside and away from the convent. Our cook, Inés, had come over by that time, and was told that a priest came out with the military detachment from La Paz, as had been the agreement between the Government and the Church, to try to assure that no atrocities would be committed by over-zealous military. Inés yelled at the priest and accused him of being a coward and traitor to his religious garb.

Some thirty armed militia had come out from La Paz, joined by the military detachment in our town of Achacachi, five tanks, and even a military plane buzzed the town. The gunfire lasted a few hours, until they finally killed one of the students, captured the two others, shot the man, and took the woman prisoner to the city.

I later learned that a friend of theirs from the university had been captured in La Paz and tortured to give five names, and so they had been forced to reveal the whereabouts of the three persons in Achacachi. The woman was imprisoned in La Paz, tortured severely, and, after a year, exiled to France.

Reprimanded and Warned

In the parish house, we tried to care for poor Inés, who by this time was hysterical from all the day's happenings. At midnight, a military guy told us that they had received orders from La Paz to bring us in to the Ministry of Interior, where they usually took political prisoners. He asked us if we had vehicles to drive ourselves. They had only one. We said yes, but we didn't have any gas.

"No problem," they replied. "We will make them open the gas station." So we gathered a few things together, negotiated to leave one of the priests to care for Inés, and drove to the central plaza to fuel up. Sure enough, they had driven one of the tanks up to the door of the gas station, shined their beacon and beat on the door until the owner came out. Of course we had to pay for our own gas to drive ourselves to jail.

On the long dark road into the city, some three hours away, we prayed and tried to figure out what they would do to us and how we could respond. We reached the city about 3:00 A.M. The bishop demanded to be released to report to the archbishop, which they agreed to do. The rest of us were ushered into the Ministry of Interior building, next to the United Nations office on Avenida Arce. They led us through winding corridors, as I wondered whether this was the place where they tortured political prisoners. They sat us down in a big room, gave us pencils and paper and told us to write down what we knew about this incident. Then they separated the priests and the Sisters, bringing us men to a small, barren room where we sat on the floor, prayed the rosary, and sang some religious songs.

About 8:00 A.M., they came for us priests and took us back through the winding corridors. The secretaries and other workers who were gathering for work looked at us with wide and suspicious eyes, as if we were terrible criminals. I noticed a newspaper on one of the desks and glanced at the headlines. It said in bold letters, "Shootout with Guerrillas at Church in Achacachi." They brought us before the minister of interior, General Adett Zamora, a heavyset man with a sinister mustache drooping over his mouth, and narrow, piercing eyes. He was very angry.

He said we had become involved in a very serious affair. Dangerous and violent people were trying to overthrow the government, he said. In Achacachi, they had captured three dangerous "guerrillas." One of the most wanted, Inti Peredo, had escaped. He had been a companion to Che Guevara in his guerrilla movement in Bolivia that the military had wiped out in 1968. We knew that was just government propaganda, but we were not in a position to argue.

He told us that we would be released, but warned us not to naively get involved in any kind of political activity. The government was in charge of the situation and was in the process of pacifying the country. We asked about the headlines that would surely disgrace our pastoral work in the area. He assured us that our names were not revealed, and we would not be implicated. That was a lie. The next day, our names were all over the papers. We asked him about the Sisters. He assured us once again that they would be similarly reprimanded and released, which was also a lie. The five Sisters who had not worked in Achacachi were in fact released, but the two other Sisters from the convent in Achacachi, Rocío and Julia Alba, were exiled back to Spain and Colombia, where they were from originally. A third Sister from the convent, Eduarda, was at home in Santa Cruz at the time. We got word to her very carefully that she was in danger, since she was a Bolivian. We urged her to seek asylum at an embassy. Actually, the apostolic nuncio, the pope's representative in Bolivia, went to Santa Cruz and accompanied her back to La Paz and immediately to asylum in the Spanish Embassy.

After the minister reprimanded us, we were shown out of the building, returned to our vehicles, which were still parked outside of the Ministry, and drove to the archbishop's office to report to him on what had happened. We also reported to our Maryknoll superiors. We then drove back out to Achacachi.

There we learned more of what had happened. The military had rounded up five of our religious leaders in town, interrogated them and subsequently confined them to a concentration camp on a cold island called Coati in the middle of Lake Titicaca. They were held there for nine months. We often reflected that the government didn't like the publicity of imprisoning priests, but they sure could persecute other lay religious workers associated with them. They had also taken prisoner the cook from the convent, and roughed her up quite a bit for information, causing her to lose several teeth.

People in town had been completely terrorized by these events, and began to look upon us with a great deal of suspicion. I wanted to address our situation and give publicly our point of view at Mass on Sunday. But the priest in charge of Achacachi, Fr. Dick Schmidburger, who had been arrested with us, forbade me from saying anything publicly. His attitude was just to let it all go and pretend that nothing had happened. I was enraged! People were being fed a bunch of lies about us as sheltering and aiding a group of violent guerrillas. We certainly had a right to defend ourselves and speak out for the sake of justice. All I could do was go around town and speak to people personally and try to explain what had happened. Many people did not want to talk to me or be seen associating with me, although several of our most faithful parishioners did receive me into their homes and courageously talked to me. I thought, this must have been how Jesus was treated toward the end of his ministry.

Standing up for Our Faith

On Sunday, I did refrain from speaking out about the incident in my sermon. But after the Mass, a number of our campesino religious leaders told me that they were being threatened for being "communists." I asked them what that meant. They said they didn't know but it sounded bad. I told them that maybe they should just lie low for a while, not say anything, and not come around the parish. Néstor Escobar, a very poor farmer, a quiet man about forty, and one of our most outstanding religious leaders, told me sternly, "No way, Father. If Jesus suffered and died for us on the cross, then the least we can do is stand up for our faith now, even though we may be persecuted." I thought, these people, simple, poor, and uneducated, have got it. They really understand what Jesus was about.

I wondered about myself in comparison to Néstor and all my pretensions. I always harbored some illusions that I might

Paul Newpower (center) saying Mass with parishioners in Achacachi, Bolivia. Fr. Gene Toland is pictured here on the left.

have some significant impact on the world or maybe on the Church or at least maybe on Maryknoll. And yet, here was Néstor, seemingly an insignificant Indian in a remote corner of the world. His friends and influence would extend to his family and a few people in his village. He, like other Aymará Indians, would be born, live, and die in a small rural farming village, so isolated from the rest of the world, in the insignificant country of Bolivia. Few people would have any awareness of their passing through this world. And yet, I thought, this poor, insignificant Néstor may seem to do so little in the eyes of the world, but is infinitely precious in the eyes of God. Would all my strivings for recognition and accomplishment gain me more than poor Néstor?

A few days later, I decided to return to La Paz and look for the five religious leaders from the town and the cook from the convent. I inquired at the police station. They asked me who I was, and I explained that I was a priest from Achacachi, looking for some of the people who had been arrested from there the previous week. The officer in charge told me that we had to go to the office of the Ministry of Interior to find out about them, and asked if I had a car. I did, so I drove back down to the place where we had been detained. He lead me through the same corridors, and we ended up in the same room where we had been detained the week before. He told me to wait. Well, I did for about an hour. Finally I asked if I could talk to someone.

They brought me before a stern-looking military guy, seated behind a large desk. He too was very angry. He told me that they had orders to arrest me if I came back into the city causing any trouble. He got up and stood over me. As I sat there in front of him, he warned me to not get involved in any way in the problems taking place in the country because it was a very complicated situation. I could go back to my parish and tend to my religious duties, but should not get involved in any political affairs. I was humiliated, intimidated, and scared, sitting there all alone before this imposing authoritative Bolivian military figure. I tried to mumble something significant in my stumbling Spanish.

Do Not Be Afraid

After a bit, the biblical passage came to me that said: "When they take you before the authorities, do not be afraid. Do not even prepare anything to say. The Holy Spirit will be your strength and speak for you." I wondered where the Holy Spirit was at that time. I guess I was just too inexperienced yet, too unprepared for that confrontation, still too timid about my faith to offer any witness against the injustices that were being committed, and to stand up for the rights of those who were being persecuted. I had gone to Achacachi to test my limits, to reach out and touch the furthest walls of my potential. But I soon learned that I had bitten off more than I could chew.

A year later, I returned to the States for my vacation, which Maryknoll granted to its missionaries every three years. I visited with a nun I knew and we talked about what I had experienced. Her response was, "Are you praying?" "Well, yeah, pretty much. Actually, sometimes," I replied. She said, "You're not going to make it if you don't spend at least an hour a day in silent prayer." She invited me to join her in prayer, and we sat there in silence for a long while. I began asking God to tell me what I should do. But the only answer that came to me was, "I am with you."

Achacachi

ACHACACHI WAS A TOWN of about four thousand people, surrounded by sixty-five Indian villages, having a population of forty thousand people. It was my second pastoral assignment in Bolivia. I had asked to go there to immerse myself further into the Indian cultures of Bolivia, but little did I know of the conflicts and challenges that were awaiting me there.

Achacachi is situated on the cold wind-swept Altiplano, at an altitude of 12,000 feet between majestic snow-covered mountains and legendary Lake Titicaca, the birthplace of the Inca empire. The area is home to the Aymará Indians, a tribe dating back three thousand years, with their own language, social structures, culture, and religion. It was all very beautiful, even enchanting, but stark and harsh in its climate. It was the ideal place for a young, hardy missionary trained for cross-cultural ministry and looking for a challenge.

Typical street market in Achacachi, Bolivia.

Dreams

WHAT INSPIRED ME to be a Maryknoll missionary and go to some far-off exotic culture? I never could figure that out. I grew up in a working-class family in St. Paul, Minnesota. I remember seeing the film *South Pacific* and being enamored with the culture of a South Sea island and felt the fascination of falling in love with a beautiful native girl. My older brother, Tom, went into the Navy and toured the Orient. One night, I dreamed of seeing him return, with a native girl on his arm. He said she was for me. Ah, the fantasies of the young. Dr. Tom Dooley wrote a book, which inspired me at the time, about his medical work among the poor in Vietnam.

But my mind was set on becoming some kind of scientist or astronomer or maybe even an astronaut. I studied physics at the University of Minnesota, but flunked out at the end of my third year. That was the end of that dream. In frustration, I took a series of vocational tests at the counseling office. The counselor told me in the evaluation that I did not share the values of physicists. I asked him who I did share values with. And he told me, with teachers or guidance counselors or people in the social field. Well, I had made a vow in high school to never teach, realizing how nasty we students were to our teachers.

My mother was quite religious, and deep down, I had a strong religious conviction, though it was not very sophisticated nor was I real pious. So I went to talk to our parish priest at the Church of Saint Casimir. I told him that I needed some guidance, and really wanted to know what the Lord wanted me to do. Of course, he immediately suggested that I become a priest. Frankly, I wasn't too impressed with old Fr. Stojyer or the other Polish priests, all dressed in their black robes, stirring momentarily among us on Sundays for Mass or in the confessional on Saturdays.

Church of St. Casimir, St. Paul, Minnesota

Nothing was working for me, so I figured I might as well just dream. I told him that I had some fantasy of joining the newly initiated Peace Corps of President John F. Kennedy and going to some far-off land to help poor people. He then suggested I become a missionary and go overseas for religious reasons. I asked him if his organization had foreign missions. And he replied that they did, in Sweden and Alaska. "Umm…any other missionary organizations around?" I replied. He told me to look in the phone book.

Contacting the Maryknoll Missionaries

I finally heard of the Maryknoll missionaries and called them in Minneapolis. They invited me over for a cookout the following Sunday. I had a million questions by now, but everyone there was just having a good time, and I really didn't have the opportunity to inquire about anything, except that I had a really good impression of some great guys with super ideals. So I called them back and made an appointment to see them. They told me it was a little late to apply for the seminary, since it was now the end of June. But I could try.

Initially I asked God to help me make a decision about the seminary and my future. As I got more interested in Maryknoll, I asked God to let me know if He wanted me to

Maryknoll Society Center, Ossining, NY

be a missionary. I guess He did because I became more excited about the prospect of actually become a foreign missionary and going to some exotic country to help poor people. And I began asking Him to let my papers go through and grant me the opportunity.

I was accepted at the last minute, but then had the task of telling my girlfriend Judy of my plans to become a celibate priest. I couldn't come up with a good way to explain that to her. So I just told her that I wanted to break up, and I walked away. She called me and insisted on talking. So finally I admitted to her my plans. She was actually supportive, though not real excited about me walking out of her life.

We continued to see each other until I left for the seminary. I used to write to her and we even got together once the next summer, but it wasn't the same. She had horses and we went for a ride. When we came back to her house, she offered me a glass of water. That was a trigger for my destiny. I had once fancied that if a girl offered me a glass of water, that would be the person for me to marry. But I got cold feet, and told myself that unfortunately I had already chosen a different track for my life.

Judy moved to Colorado, got a job at a ski resort, and married a ski instructor. Many years later on a ski trip to Vail, I stayed with some friends who knew her. We met and skied together and she introduced me to her husband, who didn't seem too excited to meet me. Years later I received a letter from her daughter, saying that she had died in a diving accident in the Caribbean. She included a postcard that Judy had written to me the day before the accident, but never mailed.

Seminary

THE MARYKNOLL COLLEGE SEMINARY was located near Chicago. My folks and younger brother Don drove me there. My mother was very pleased that I would be studying to become a priest. But my father was more dubious. He thought I should have finished college first, to have something to fall back on if the seminary didn't work out. In the end, he said, whatever you feel you need to do. After they drove away and left me, I lay in my dorm bed and cried, my first time to leave home and start a new life, with very little idea of what I was getting into.

The seminary was bursting at its seams in 1962. Mary-

Maryknoll College, Glen Ellyn, Illinois, c. 1963

knoll had just doubled the size of the facilities to accommodate the six hundred young men studying for the priesthood. It was an amazing group of idealistic, tough, friendly, intelligent young men, and being a part of them excited me tremendously. We all dreamed of going to some far-off country, becoming involved in different cultures, and hopefully helping poor people in their needs. Those were formative years for a young man, just out of St. Paul, Minnesota, with hardly a clue as to what was happening in the world, just inspired by President Kennedy's words of "Ask not what your country can do for you, but what you can do for your country." I read some *Maryknoll* magazines and was romantically attracted to a picture of a priest standing behind a group of Japanese children eating watermelons. I thought, I could be that guy, serving those beautiful children somewhere in the Orient.

The seminary was quite traditional and strict at the time. We were allowed visitors one Sunday a month, and infrequently were allowed off property. Our lives were taken up with studies, religious practices, and sports.

Beyond the Sacred Walls

The seminary training included involvement in some ministry or service outside of the sacred walls. A group of us were sent to the inner city of Chicago to get exposed to poor people and the experience of Church in a Black neighborhood. That was my first experience outside of a white community. We were asked to help take a census of the parish, to go around knocking on doors and inquiring about people interested in the Catholic Church. The priest gave me directions on the area of the parish he wanted me to cover, and off I went, a little nervous about this first venture out alone in a very strange environment. I walked one block and got completely lost and disoriented. A Black man noticed me and probably sensed my bewilderment. He came over and started talking to me. I told him my dilemma, he laughed and pointed me in the right direction. With that friendly first encounter, I was suddenly all right. It surprised me to find that these strange people, whom I had only seen from afar, were so cordial and friendly to me. Feeling my courage, I knocked on the door of one house that seemed almost abandoned. No one answered downstairs, so I climbed the rickety steps to the second floor. Still no answer. I tried on the third floor, and could hear muffled voices inside. They didn't answer. I kept knocking. Finally a voice came from within, "Who that?" I answered that I was from the local Catholic Church and wanted to talk to them. They replied, "Ain't nobody home." "What?" I said. "Ain't nobody home here," came the reply again.

A Fire Is Ignited

That little ministry ignited a fire in me for the struggles of the Black community at the time, and I later had the opportunity to hear Dr. Martin Luther King Jr. give one of his famous speeches at Soldier Field in Chicago. Eight years earlier, in 1955, Rosa Parks, a courageous Black woman, refused to give up her seat on a bus and was arrested. That started the whole nonviolent movement of Black people in the South for integration. The reaction was not so nonviolent. In 1963, in Birmingham, Alabama, four Black children were blown up in a church. The following year, three civil rights workers would be assassinated in Mississippi. Finally that year, the US Congress passed the landmark Civil Rights Act, which guaranteed the rights of all citizens, including Blacks, and legally ended segregation, but not in practice. Doctor King would be assassinated four years later, April 4, 1968.

According to the seminary schedule, we were to have morning prayers before breakfast, and evening prayers after supper, all together in the large chapel. We recited the prayers and sang the ancient Gregorian chant melodies of the Psalms out of a huge, thick book called the *Liber Usualis*, the "useful book" in Latin. Often the prayers were routine and boring. But sometimes the rhythm would lull me into like a trance. One night, after most everyone else had rushed out of the chapel, I lingered in a quiet peacefulness. I felt a presence near me, like right above and in front of me. I remained enraptured in the feeling for quite a while, until someone began shutting off all the lights. I was all alone and it was time to be in our rooms.

One of the required courses was psychology, taught by Fr. Gene Kennedy. He was an excellent teacher, and encouraged us to receive some personal counseling as a part of our formation. So I went to see him one evening. I stammered around to try to say something about my feelings. But when I looked up, he was sleeping. That didn't do much good for my self-esteem, but it was the start of a long process of introspection.

War in Vietnam

President Kennedy was assassinated that year. The age of innocence was quickly coming to an end. President Johnson began heating up the Vietnam War, and we seminarians were shocked to hear that an ex-Maryknoll seminarian from the class ahead of us had been one of the first to burn his draft card in protest of the war. Maryknoll was raising our consciousness and giving us courage to act on our beliefs.

A young man followed me at the seminary, Roy Bourgeois. Roy had been a lieutenant in the Navy, served in Vietnam, and received a Purple Heart for wounds sustained there. Seeing the work of a priest in Vietnam caring for orphans of war, Roy decided to become a priest. He was a good-looking, robust young man with an endearing southern drawl, a great role model for young idealistic people. Maryknoll sent him on the road to recruit young men for the Maryknoll priesthood from high schools and colleges. Roy talked, of course, about his experience in Vietnam and how proud he had been

Navy lieutenant Roy Bourgeois receiving the Purple Hart from Admiral N.G. Ward.

to serve his country. But now he wanted to do the same for God. He continually got barraged with questions about the war, about the pretensions of the United States, and his own convictions. Gradually Roy began to reconsider his position and he grew to become a radical critic of the Vietnam war. He ended up returning his Purple Heart medal to the Pentagon and organizing veterans against the war, all the while continuing his seminary studies. Later, he would be assigned to Bolivia. There our paths would intertwine.

After graduating from college in 1964 with a degree in philosophy, I spent a summer in Berea, Kentucky, in a project run by Fr. Ralph Beiting. We were housed in a small cabin in a rural area, with the warning that this was Ku Klux Klan territory, and that they did not look kindly on do-gooders from the north who came down to help the "niggers." Great introduction! That night we were awakened by gunshots and shouting. We saw a cross burning outside our door. Our first night in KKK land and we were scared stiff. The young directors of the program burst through the door and let out a great laugh at how they had scared us half to death.

In the fall my folks drove me to the Maryknoll Novitiate near Boston, where we seminarians spent a quiet year to discern further our vocations.

Then it was on to theological studies for four years at the Maryknoll major seminary among the rolling hills of Westchester County, north of New York City. The seminary was an exciting place, with real-live missionaries returning from Africa, Asia, and Latin America. They frequently shared their stories with us. That time awakened me to the world. I became particularly interested in Latin America, because of the revolutionary changes taking place there, and the dramatic reversal of the Catholic Church from supporting the rich landowners to siding with the poor in their struggles for justice and a decent life.

■

Pastoral Experiences

ONE SUMMER VACATION a group of us seminarians took an apartment in Harlem on 114th Street, at the suggestion of the local Catholic Church. At the time it was still possible for a group of do-gooder middle-class white folks to do that. We simply sought to get to know the people on the block, provide some recreational activities for the children, and be a presence of the Catholic Church in their midst. For the first time, I felt like an outsider, a minority in the midst of a culture and society that I was not a part of nor understood. The streets were always alive with many, many people, just getting out of their oven-like apartments, and socializing with one another. Kids were playing all over the place. We took a group of the children on an outing, on what we thought might be an interesting excursion up to Morningside Heights, near Columbia University. We climbed a series of steps up out of Harlem and emerged into the strange and quiet world of tall, clean apartment buildings. No one was on the streets. The kids said to me, "Let's get out of here." I asked why. They said, "This is scary. There ain't nobody around. We want to go home."

Not far from Maryknoll's major seminary in Ossining, NY, was Marymount College, a private college then exclusively for women. Several of us seminarians sought to broaden our experiences with foreign students, to get to know their cultures and mentalities. So we organized activities with several foreign students there, from Japan, India, and countries in Latin America. One of the students was Monica, daughter of the mayor of Kyoto, Japan. Monica told me of her difficulty in becoming fluent enough in English to complete her studies. She had become depressed, on the verge of suicide, and as a distraction, stayed up all night making origami paper figures of a bird of peace. The next day she gave them all to one of the elderly nuns convalescing in the hospital. And suddenly Monica recovered, and felt reassured to continue struggling with her new culture and language.

I became enamored with Monica, and we developed a special friendship, well, actually we fell in love. One day Monica asked me what she could tell her father. I got scared. My intentions were to continue on in the seminary, get ordained, and go to Latin America. Our relationship dampened, but after seminary, when she went back to Japan, we continued to correspond. Years later I had the opportunity to visit Japan to do a film and looked her up. We spent a pleasant, but awkward day touring Tokyo. In the evening, I wondered what to say as we departed. Monica handed me an envelope, shook my hand, and we separated. The envelope contained all the letters I had sent her over the years.

In the Air

At Christmas, we were obligated to stay at the seminary through Midnight Mass on Christmas Eve, and then were free on vacation for two weeks. At two in the morning, four of us headed for the airport. A couple of the seminarians had become licensed pilots and had bought a small plane. They were flying out to Chicago and invited me to go along.

It was a crisp,

Terry Cedar (left) and members of the "Flying Club" in Maryknoll's major seminary.

dark night as we climbed into the small craft and buckled in. The strip was icy and we veered off the runway as we were about to take off. Fortunately, no harm was done, but it made me wonder about the flying ability of my seminarian companions. We stopped to refuel at a small airport in the middle of the night and took off once again into the darkness.

Up in the air, it was pitch black. Even looking down, few lights could be seen. It was as if we were floating in a deep, black sea. Suddenly the motor quit! The two pilots frantically began pulling switches and pushing buttons. Now I was really scared! "What's happening?" I said frightfully, as the plane glided down through the total darkness in total silence. They didn't know. Maybe we would be lucky and land on a highway or roadway. Just as suddenly the motor started again, and once again we began gaining altitude. Now I was mad. What had these two rookies gotten me into? I just wanted an inexpensive way to get to Chicago and St. Paul for the holidays. We located another county airport and landed, to discover that the fuel attendant at the last airport had not replaced the cap of the gasoline tank on one of the wings. Fortunately, we were using that tank first, and when it ran out, we were able to switch over to the other full tank on the other wing.

It wasn't over yet. As morning broke, we needed to refuel again. By this time we were over Ohio. So they radioed in to the Cleveland airport to request landing permission. The tower told them to look for a beacon and some tall build-

Accidents will happen. Some of Maryknoll's "trusty pilots" encountered rough weather on occasion. Happily everyone survived in this particular mishap in Croton-on-Hudson, near Maryknoll's major seminary.

ings. Hmm. Our trusty pilots couldn't locate them. The tower asked them what they could see. They described a few light patterns. The response came back, "You jerks are over Akron, not Cleveland." Next stop was Chicago, and I was relieved to leave my flying companions and board a train for St. Paul.

1968: A Turbulent Year

The following year, 1968, was not a good year. In April, Martin Luther King Jr. was assassinated. In June, Bobby Kennedy was killed. In Bolivia, Che Guevara was killed, trying to start a liberation movement among the poor. And in December, Fr. Thomas Merton, a Trappist monk, a brilliant spiritual writer who had a significant influence on my life, died accidentally of electrocution while visiting Thailand.

After a freewheeling youth, Thomas Merton had had a conversion experience and entered the monastery in 1941, the year I was born. In spite of living as a monk or hermit, he was a prolific writer and authored many books on spirituality and commentaries on society and social issues. Early on he perceived the banality of the Vietnam War. Early on he perceived the lunacy and danger of the nuclear arms race. He endorsed the civil rights movement of Dr. King. All the while, he developed a deep spiritual basis for living more humanly and fulfilling our God-given potentials.

Life on the Streets of Chicago

The summer of 1968, after being ordained to the diaconate ministry at Maryknoll, I traveled to Chicago to participate in the Urban Training Center for Christian Mission. The Ecumenical Center sponsored a three-month in-depth experience in an inner-city ministry. The directors told us that our first experience would be "The Plunge," seven days living on the streets of Chicago with only five dollars in our pockets. They offered us some tips on where to hang out, to find a job or a place to sleep. I let my beard grow and put on some older clothes, ruffled up my hair, and took a bus downtown.

I got off near the Salvation Army Mission for homeless people. Standing on a street corner, a Black guy came up to me and started talking. He told me he knew karate and showed me how hard the side of his hand was. He took a couple of swipes at me, laughing. He invited me to buy a bottle of wine and go with him to see some friends, which we did. He said that he slept under some steps way down in one of the subway tunnels, where no one would bother him. I could join him if I needed a place to stay. Then he dragged me into a bar. Heck, I was spending all my five bucks. When he was distracted talking to some other guys, I slipped out the door, and hurried away in the night, back to the Salvation Army Mission.

Many men were gathering in the conference hall and I took a seat. A man dressed in a ruffled suit took the podium and started preaching to us. He said he too had been dirty, disheveled, and lost on the streets. But he discovered the Lord and was saved from his sinfulness. "Now look at me," he said. "I wear a suit, I'm clean, have a job, and am saved." Then he came out into the congregation with his Bible. He offered it to me to read. It was the parable of the rich man and Lazarus. I read it. Then he took the Bible, returned to the podium and said, "Look at that wretched man under the table. He is like all of you, not working and begging for scraps. You could be like the gentleman sitting at the table eating decently, if you would only accept the Lord as your savior, change your lives and be saved." Then he asked, "Who of you wants to be saved?" The guy next to me said, "Tell him you want to be, and they will call you first to the food line." He stood up and said, "I sure do, preacher." And the preacher called him up and gave him a meal ticket. Well, I wasn't quite up to that, so I just waited until all the saved people went downstairs to eat, and then the preacher handed out meal tickets to all of us stragglers and sinners.

Actually, the Salvation Army does an incredible service to take in all these men, give them a meal and a place to sleep. The food wasn't bad. And after, they lined us up, stripped us naked, and ran us through a hot shower. Afterwards, they gave us a clean nightshirt and showed us to our dormitories. We each had a separate bed, but the hacking coughs of all the other men in the room kept me awake all night. The next morning we were roused, given our clothes back, fed breakfast, and allowed to return to the streets.

 I wandered about, looking at all the nicely dressed people, and wondered what they thought of me. I figured I'd better try to get a job and make some money, if I didn't want to return to the Salvation Army Mission that night. A day-laborer office had a line of people waiting, so I joined them for the opportunity. They took the white guys first, and passed over the Black and Hispanic guys. We were sent to a factory to glue cardboard boxes together. The glue stuck to my hands and smelled awful. At the end of the day, I had $10 in my pocket, and felt rich. I went to a bar and had a drink. The waitress came by with a second, which I politely refused. She insisted, saying that there was a two drink minimum. Darn, there went half of my salary.

 That night I thought I would just sleep in a park. It was early yet as I sat there with nothing to do and nowhere to go. A guy came by and sat down next to me and started talking. Then he asked if I didn't want to join him and his friend for a few drinks at his apartment, as he reached over and tried to stroke my cheek. Not my cup of tea, and I was out of there. A park is not a safe place to sleep alone at night. You don't know who might mug you. So I just walked around all night, and then dozed on a park bench the next morning for a while. More walking the streets, wondering about people like myself except they were really without any resources or hope.

 That night I took a room in a cheap hotel. The next day I went looking for work. There was a sign for temporary employment so I went in. I heard the guy behind the desk tell a fat lady that she had to put $20 down to get a job. Forget it. I didn't have that kind of money, and got up to leave. The guy behind the desk saw me start to leave and came out. "Hold on, son. Where are you going," he asked. I told him I didn't have $20 to put up for a job. He told me that we could arrange something, and he invited me into his office. He asked me what I was doing. I told him that I was just passing through Chicago and needed a job for a day to get some money. He looked at me and said, "Son, you look like you are at the end of your rope. Get yourself together. Why not settle down for a while. I have a good job for you landscaping for a rich family. But you would have to live there and stay there for a couple of months, at least." I thanked him for his genuine concern for me, but told him I was moving on. He seemed really sorry to see me leave the office.

At the end of the "plunge" experience, we all gathered back at the Urban Training Center for a debriefing. Some of the people had done pretty well out on the streets, did some gambling and even made some money. Others really couldn't take it and returned early.

Community Organizing on Chicago's South Side

My assignment for the rest of the summer was at a community organization in a changing neighborhood on the South Side of Chicago. The other people in the organization had all been trained by Saul Alinsky in the principles of organizing a neighborhood to achieve its concerns. In this case, it was absentee landlords, renting out their old buildings to whomever came along, and not caring for the upkeep of the neighborhood. We spent the summer knocking on doors, asking people their opinions, looking for community leaders, and trying to build a consensus on how to act for their concerns. At the end, we organized a meeting of all the neighbors to motivate the leaders we found and to form a community organization that would fight with the force of everyone united, marching, petitioning, demanding to be heard by the politicians.

At the end of the summer, I bought a 1954 "Oldsmobile 98" for fifty dollars, changed the oil pump that was leaking, and drove to St. Paul to see my folks. The Olds ran so well, except for guzzling lots of gas, that I drove it all the way back to New York. I used it all during my final year in the seminary.

■

Formation for Mission

RETURNING TO THE SEMINARY in September 1968, we were surprised to find out that our rector, Fr. George Weber (who was in charge of the seminary and our religious formation), had left the priesthood and married a Maryknoll Sister. George had been an outstanding missionary in Africa and he often shared stories of his experiences there. As rector, he was an unassuming, spiritual, and pious man. He always gave great sermons, especially about celibacy. During the next decade hundreds of Maryknoll missionaries would similarly leave the ministry and get married, including Fr. John McCormack, the superior general of all the Maryknoll priests and Brothers in the world. The best always seemed to be leaving, we would say.

My formation was enriched and strengthened by the witnesses and writings of people like Dorothy Day, the radical founder of the Catholic Worker Movement, by Dr. Martin Luther King Jr. in his nonviolent Christian movement, by Br. Charles de Foucauld, a French ex-military who left everything to witness to the poor in northern Africa, where he was martyred. Fr. Thomas Price, one of the founders of Maryknoll in 1918, also inspired me in a strange way. He was a rather traditional old priest, working among the poor in the hills of South Carolina. His spirit of poverty impressed me. He seemed so detached from worldly goods and worldly ambitions. And he had a zeal to reach out to those in need, those untouched by the Church or neglected by society.

Also several non-Catholic people deeply inspired me at the time: Henry David Thoreau wrote about a simple lifestyle in Walden, Massachusetts. Dag Hammarskjöld, the second secretary general of the United Nations from 1953 until 1961 and a Christian mystic, wrote a deeply personal and spiritual account of his commitment to world peace and development, called *Markings*. He was honored with a Nobel Peace Prize. In 1961, while trying to mediate a conflict in northern Rhodesia, now Zimbabwe, his plane mysteriously crashed and he was killed.

Another inspiration for me was Mahatma Gandhi, one of the greatest spiritual leaders of the century. He developed and realized a life of prayerful non-violent confrontation with an oppressive British colonial power in India. In 1948, he too was assassinated, as seems to be the fate of radical, spiritual, socially minded prophets.

Seminary training whetted my appetite for social activism and for a deeper spirituality. Frankly, I never felt real comfortable with the more dogmatic teachings that had developed down through the history of the Church. I loved Scripture, which seemed so much closer to the actual life of Jesus. Nor did I feel comfortable with the clericalism of a privileged class, separated from the general life of the laity. But priesthood in Maryknoll was the way to be a missionary, and that's what I wanted most of all.

It was 1969. Che Guevara had been killed the year before, trying to start a revolution in Bolivia.. The same year, two Maryknoll priests, Tom and Arthur Melville and Maryknoll Sister Margarita Bradford were expelled from Guatemala for their sympathy with the Mayan Indian guerrillas who were trying to overthrow a genocidal government in that country. Tom later wrote a book entitled *Through a Glass Darkly: The U.S. Holocaust in Central America*, detailing the oppression of the Mayan Indians. I have to admit to a romanticized notion of revolution at the time. Only later in Bolivia did I come to realize the actual cost of bloodshed among innocent people.

The Church in the United States at the time sponsored an annual conference called Cicop, bringing many prominent and progressive Church leaders from Latin America to educate us US Catholics about their dramatic participation in movements for the liberation of the poor. At one Cicop conference I heard Bishop Hélder Câmara from Recife, Brazil, say, "If you give food to the poor, people say you are so charitable. But if you ask why the poor have no bread, they call you a communist." And that's exactly the reputation this little man, who reminded me of Mr. Magoo, gained in his country. Years later, I had the opportunity to accompany him for a few days in New York. I was deeply touched by his humble spirituality.

Vatican II

We were privileged in the seminary to be studying theology shortly after the Second Vatican Council had ended in 1965, dramatically refocusing the Church to become much more relevant to society in the twenty-first century. The bishops, who had gathered from around the world, stated in a document called "The Church in the Modern World": "The joys and the hopes, the grief and anxieties of the people of this age, especially those who are poor or in any way afflicted, are the joys and hopes, the grief and anxieties of the followers of Christ." We were told that the Church was no longer to be considered a hierarchical institution patterned after monarchical governments, but rather as a much more participative model, the People of God. We were instructed that now Religious should become more involved in the daily lives of common people and especially active in meeting the needs of the poor. The bishops emphasized two important values: the inherent and inviolable dignity of each person and the unity of all humanity as brothers and sisters. They stressed the interdependence of all nations and all peoples long before the age of globalization. An essential part of our task was now to actively promote the equality and common good of all peoples, rather than leave that to unregulated economic systems.

Medellín Conference

The bishops of Latin America, who had helped form those documents, met in Medellín, Colombia, in 1968 and ran with those inspirations. They produced an outstanding and quite revolutionary document of their own, calling the Church in Latin America, of which I would be a part, to "make a preferential option for the poor." And calling the injustices experienced by the majority of peoples in Latin America, such as hunger, an institutionalized violence against them. The upper classes of most of Latin America had been used to preferential treatment from the Church, in exchange for monetary support, respect, and political power. Now they felt that the Church was betraying them, switching sides and taking up the cause of the poor. This document became a rallying point for a significant sector of the Church in Latin America and, unknown to me at the time, an inspiration for the development a few years later, of Liberation Theology, a reinterpretation of scripture unique to Latin America.

For my theological degree from Maryknoll, I wrote my thesis on the Medellín Conference of Latin American bishops and the popular education movements of Paulo Freire in Brazil. Freire was starting a peaceful revolution, educating poor people to read with emotional words like bread, food, work, and stimulating people to talk about those words and what they meant to them. He had developed a whole philosophy and methodology for helping poor people to learn to read and write, which included a process to promote their own liberation.

Medellín, Colombia

Ordination for Bolivia

TWENTY OF US WERE ORDAINED in 1969, the year Richard Nixon became president. Most were sent to countries in Asia, Africa, and Latin America. Full of enthusiasm for adventure and commitment to the Gospel, each of us hoped ours would be a lifetime of spreading the Good News of Jesus Christ and service to those in need. Little did we know of our personal destinies, how the experiences would change us, and where they would lead us. But we were foolish for Christ and willing to take the chance and the risk. Lifetime celibacy did not sound great to me at the time, but heck, maybe the pope would change that in the future. I even left behind the six-inch reflector telescope I had ground and made by hand, following the example of Saint Francis of Assisi to leave everything behind, and of Dorothy Day, who said, "The best thing to do with the best things you have, is to give them away." I sure missed that telescope many years later.

MARYKNOLL
ordination and departure ceremonies
1969

Why foreign mission? There was always a sense of adventure, to go on a pilgrimage, to leave behind my previous life and embark on a journey into the unknown, to go to a faraway place, a sacred

Departure 1969

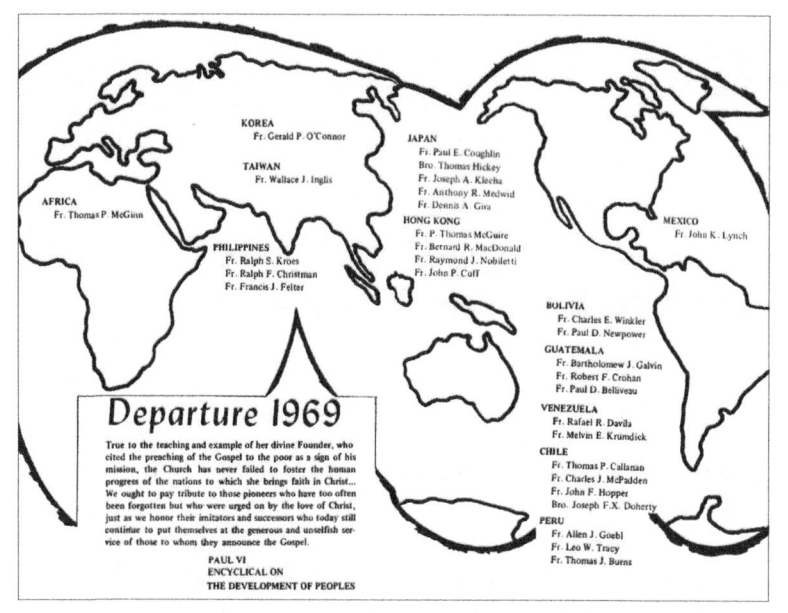

True to the teaching and example of her divine Founder, who cited the preaching of the Gospel to the poor as a sign of his mission, the Church has never failed to foster the human progress of the nations to which she brings faith in Christ... We ought to pay tribute to those pioneers who have too often been forgotten but who were urged on by the love of Christ, just as we honor their imitators and successors who today still continue to put themselves at the generous and unselfish service of those to whom they announce the Gospel.

PAUL VI
ENCYCLICAL ON
THE DEVELOPMENT OF PEOPLES

KOREA
Fr. Gerald P. O'Connor

TAIWAN
Fr. Wallace J. Inglis

AFRICA
Fr. Thomas P. McGinn

PHILIPPINES
Fr. Ralph S. Kroes
Fr. Ralph F. Christman
Fr. Francis J. Felter

JAPAN
Fr. Paul E. Coughlin
Bro. Thomas Hickey
Fr. Joseph A. Kleeha
Fr. Anthony R. Medwid
Fr. Dennis A. Gira

HONG KONG
Fr. P. Thomas McGuire
Fr. Bernard R. MacDonald
Fr. Raymond J. Nobiletti
Fr. John P. Cuff

MEXICO
Fr. John K. Lynch

BOLIVIA
Fr. Charles E. Winkler
Fr. Paul D. Newpower

GUATEMALA
Fr. Bartholomew J. Galvin
Fr. Robert F. Crohan
Fr. Paul D. Belliveau

VENEZUELA
Fr. Rafael R. Davila
Fr. Melvin E. Krumdick

CHILE
Fr. Thomas P. Callanan
Fr. Charles J. McPadden
Fr. John F. Hopper
Bro. Joseph F.X. Doherty

PERU
Fr. Allen J. Goebl
Fr. Leo W. Tracy
Fr. Thomas J. Burns

Members of Paul's ordination class (1969) were assigned to Maryknoll missions in Latin America, Asia, and Africa. Paul and Fr. Charles Winkler were assigned to Bolivia.

place, and hopefully on the journey to discover new aspects of my own deeper self and the face of God. It is a disconcerting movement filled with anxiety...to renounce what seems most dear in an attempt to find something even more profound, more dear, more meaningful, more worthwhile. St. Augustine once said, "My heart is restless until it rests with you, my God."

A Restless Heart

There was also a desire to put myself in a situation where I would be confronted with others who were vastly different from me, to learn from them how they viewed the world and God. Ultimately, it was a desire to share in the hopes and sufferings and struggles of humanity for a far-better world, for us now and for future generations.

I still feel the restlessness. But at the same time, I feel I'm closer to the truth, on the right path. Glimmers of fulfillment have truly stirred my soul over the years, given me profound

Paul Newpower and classmate Tom Burns wearing their mission crosses on Departure Day, Maryknoll, NY, June 1969.

Paul Newpower, Ordination Day, 24 May 1969

joy and a sense of peace that I have not found in all the enticements that society has to offer.

Bolivia was to be my destiny, as determined by the Maryknoll superiors. They passed over my first choices of Chile and Peru, which I thought at the time were much more revolutionary countries.

Bill Lafferty

A missionary from Bolivia was visiting Maryknoll at the time, Fr. Bill Lafferty, and I was anxious to find out something about the country that would soon become my new home. Actually, Bill was then taking a leave from Maryknoll to get married in Bolivia.

We later would become fast friends in Bolivia. He had a piece of land in Mizque, about six hours from Cochabamba and years later invited me to go dove hunting with him there. After a futile day we met back at a clearing, and suddenly some doves fluttered up before us. Bill raised his gun and it went off, striking me in the leg with fifty small pellets. Amid his apologies, we applied a tourniquet and hobbled an hour back to his house. There we mounted his motorcycle and began another half-hour journey to town. The pain now became intense, but we still had to dismount and jump on stones across a stream. Finally at the clinic in Mizque, the doctor cleaned the wound and told me I would have to go to a hospital back in Cochabamba for an operation to remove the pellets. "Fine. I'll go tomorrow." The doctor told me that the next train to Cochabamba would not leave for three days. That evening, I had to take a pee. The bathroom was outside and five doors away. The pain was fierce, so I decided to try to just make it to the sink in my room. I got there and leaned on it to relieve myself, and the sink ripped off the wall. But I'm getting way ahead of myself.

Paul (left) is pictured here in 2010 with Bill Lafferty and Bill's wife, Carlota. Dudley Conneely (center) holds a grandchild of the Laffertys.

Bill shared with me that Bolivia is a small, poor country, in the heart of Latin America and is insignificant to the modern world. I thought, well if Jesus were to return, he would probably chose a country like Bolivia, so similar to Palestine at the time, poor, insignificant, and at the margin of the powerful Roman Empire. My ideal was to follow the example of Jesus, who chose to be born into a poor, working-class family, live up-country in Galilee, far from Jerusalem, the center of power. To all appearances, Jesus was an insignificant carpenter and his life would be insignificant—to his family, to his country, to his Jewish religion, and to the world, losing himself in service to others rather than seeking fame or personal wealth.

■

Bolivia and Latin America

AND SO BEGAN MY PILGRIMAGE TO BOLIVIA, though I did not know anything about a pilgrimage at the time. The country I arrived in was in turmoil. I saw six presidents come and go during my first two years, mostly through military coups.

Priests were also leaving the ministry in droves. The two succeeding superiors of Maryknoll in Bolivia left to get married shortly after my arrival, and a couple of years later, one of the priests who arrived with me left and married a local Bolivian woman.

Had the thought crossed my mind? Sure! Bolivian women were quite friendly to us exuberant North Americans, eager to speak some Spanish, get to know the culture and explore our new surroundings. The fact that we were priests seemed to give them a sense of security that we were not on the make. Meanwhile, we new arrivals were struggling with culture shock. The frustration of not being able to communicate and feelings of inadequacy about how to act in society produced a sense of insecurity and alienation. We were good targets for a sweet Bolivian woman to hold our hands and reassure us that everything was all right.

Language School in Cochabamba
My first six months I spent tucked away at the excellent Maryknoll Language Institute in Cochabamba, learning Spanish.

The Maryknoll Language Institute in Cochabamba, Bolivia.

At Christmas, a couple of us priests traveled to the Amazon in the far northern part of Bolivia. Maryknoll had started its mission in Bolivia in 1942 with an outpost in the little jungle town of Riberalta. Their work was to ply the many rivers of the vast area visiting little villages, settlements, and isolated jungle tribes with the Word of God, sacraments, and medicines. They established a radio for people to communicate messages to families and relatives scattered throughout the jungle and to organize cooperatives to commercialize their rubber and Brazil nuts, avoiding the middle-men who would fleece them for profits.

Language school students taking some time off. Paul Newpower is second from the right on the ground.

The veteran missionaries there loaded me on a chug boat to go up river a couple of days and celebrate Christmas Masses in several isolated villages. Arriving at our destination, we had to trudge through the steaming-hot jungle for another couple of hours, lugging the large suitcase that contained the vestments and chalice to celebrate Mass. When we finally reached the first town, I was soaking wet with sweat and covered in bites from mosquitoes and *mariwi*. Opening the suitcase, I discovered that the priests had loaded me down with a large altar stone and a full bottle of wine. My Spanish was mediocre, but the jungle people appreciated my visit and the chance to celebrate Christmas Mass.

They told me of a previous visit by a priest. He came in a long dugout canoe, sitting at the far back end. He noticed the people on shore waving to him and thought they were excited to welcome him. When he arrived at the village, the people told him that a big snake had come out of the water and tried to strike him on the back. Fortunately he wore a leather jacket and was leaning forward, stretching the leather across his back, and the snake couldn't get a bite of him.

"How big do the snakes get here?" I asked. They told me that one of the villagers had a big German Shepherd dog. The dog was barking one night and suddenly the barking stopped. The next day the man went looking for his dog, and found a huge boa constrictor sleeping with a huge lump at one point in his fifteen-foot-long body. The snake had swallowed the dog whole.

Back at the language school, I became friends with one of my teachers, a young college graduate by the name of Ignacio Soto. He was a handsome guy with a winning smile and a wonderfully warm personality. We became friends. We often talked politics and I came to appreciate his progressive ideals for a just society with a more equal distribution of wealth. Outside of classes he worked with a cooperative to help poor families with low-interest loans. A few years later, during the Banzer dictatorship in Bolivia, he escaped to Chile to avoid persecution for his progressive ideas.

Reign of the Dictators

At the time Chile was still a free society under the socialist president, Salvador Allende. But shortly afterward, the CIA and the US government got scared that Chile might be following the way of Cuba and began to subvert the Chilean government. They promoted General Augusto Pinochet in his efforts to stage a coup and overthrow the democratically elected government. It was a bloody coup in 1973. Protesters were shot at close range. Thousands of dissenters were rounded up in the soccer stadium and later tortured for information or killed. A couple of Maryknoll priests were caught in the repression but fortunately were released. This horrible page of history was depicted in 1983 in an excellent movie *Missing*, starring Jack Lemmon. The movie documented the disappearance of a US reporter, and the frustrated efforts of his father to find him as he slowly began to realize that his own government had no interest at all in exposing the cruelty of their newly established government.

Pinochet formed a secret network with the other dictatorships in Bolivia, Argentina, Uruguay, Brazil, and Paraguay called "Project Condor." This operation would share names of political dissidents and

Bolivia's Hugh Banzer is pictured on the left (top) and on the right (bottom) with Chilean dicator General Augusto Pinochet.

if they surfaced in another country, they would be arrested, interrogated, and imprisoned. My friend, Ignacio Soto, fell within the pale of Project Condor. In 1974, word came back to Bolivia that he had been arrested in Chile and during detention jumped out of a window and killed himself. No one believed that. Obviously he had been tortured and killed by the Pinochet dictatorship.

Ignacio's body was brought back to Cochabamba and his family had a Mass said for his burial at the Maryknoll parish of Santa Ana. I so much wanted to say that Mass and speak up for my friend. But the pastor, a graying conservative old Maryknoll priest, routinely performed the rite, with no personal reference to this courageous visionary who had given his life for the poor.

Pinochet ruled Chile with an iron hand until 1990, supported over the years by Nixon, Kissinger, Reagan, and Margaret Thatcher. During that time his government killed thirty-three hundred people branded as subversives. Another million were driven into exile, saving their lives.

Argentina experienced an even more savage dictatorial government during the years from 1973 until 1982 under General Rafael Videla. During his "dirty war" some thirty thousand people were cruelly tortured and assassinated as supposed communist sympathizers and opponents of the government.

Brazil, Uruguay, and Paraguay also experienced similar cruel Gestapo-type dictatorships during that time. In all, during the 1970s and 1980s in Latin America, almost a million civilians—those the military governments did not consider loyal to their plans—were rounded up, tortured, and assassinated. This number included thousands of lay religious leaders, almost a hundred priests and nuns, and several bishops. More people were killed for their faith during that time in Latin America than all the martyrs recognized by the Church during the first three centuries of Christianity.

Washington's Role

Why the wave of harsh dictators in Latin America during the

1970s and 1980s? After the Cuban revolution in 1959, in which Fidel Castro established a communist government in America's backyard, the United States feared more countries in the hemisphere would follow Castro's lead. Progressive governments were democratically elected in Brazil, Chile, Uruguay, Argentina, and Bolivia. Those governments were nationalistic in character, meaning that they were concerned about national sovereignty, control of their own resources, and independence from foreign intervention in domestic political affairs. In a word, running their countries as they saw fit for the advantage of their own people. Unfortunately, Washington viewed those governments as potentially communist and thought they needed to be replaced by ones more congenial to US interests. The alternative to left-leaning governments was right-wing military governments that had no qualms about suppressing dissidents, communists, socialists, or anyone else suspected of criticizing the military regimes. In the eyes of the United States, a strong military government, even though it may have been brutal toward its citizens and dismissive of human rights, was much preferable to a leftist government, sympathetic to Castro, soft on communism, and critical of US economic interests in the hemisphere.

■

La Paz, Bolivia

AFTER FINISHING LANGUAGE SCHOOL in February of 1970, I moved to La Paz, the unofficial capital of Bolivia situated high in the Andes at a dizzying 12,000 feet. A Bolivian family with three university students rented me a room, which gave me the opportunity to speak Spanish all the time. It turned out that the father of the family was a colonel in the military. His wife once told me of a conversation at a military reception. Another ranking officer asked the colonel why he stayed in Bolivia. He suggested the colonel take a post in Venezuela or someplace else, make a far better salary, and live a much more comfortable life. Bolivia was going nowhere, he said. The wife of the colonel was quite scandalized at a military officer who was supposed to be patriotic and defending the country. But alas, most of the military, I was to learn, were in it for power and prestige. They could care less about the fate of Bolivia. Subsequent military governments proved that all too true.

Next door lived a young college professor and political scientist from England. I asked him why he chose to come to Bolivia. He told me that as a political scientist from Europe you could understand all the political systems in Latin America, except Bolivia. It was so unique and complicated that you had to live here to understand it. Added to that were the complex social organization and cultural values of the majority indigenous population.

The young man at the house where I was staying, Alex,

once asked if I wanted to go to a movie the following Saturday. This was the first time that he was including me in his social life, and I was anxious to participate. Saturday came and I waited for him to tell me the time we would be leaving. I waited and waited. He never showed up. The next day I asked him what happened. We were supposed to go to a movie. He said casually without an apology, "Oh, I was with my girlfriend." After similar frustrations of people inviting me out and then not showing up, I began to realize that a polite social custom in Bolivia was to tell people you would like to get together, with no intention of actually doing so. To be sure of an invitation, one has to specify a time, and emphasize that it is a firm commitment. I later got into it. When my folks visited a few years later, we met a friend of mine on the street. He said give me call tomorrow and we can get together. I told him, sure. My mom reminded me that we were not going to be in town tomorrow. But I reassured her that it was only a polite intention that neither one of us had any intention of fulfilling.

Culture Shock

The culture shock that I continually experienced was quite normal for a foreigner transplanted into a strange new world. I began to feel what it was like to be an immigrant and thought that my grandparents must have felt all of that same alienation, confusion, and inadequacy when they went to the USA from Poland, Ukraine, and Czechoslovakia. They compensated by living in a ghetto of similar people, leaving adapting to the new culture and language to their children. Unlike them, I wanted to immerse myself in the new culture on my own and learn the new language as fast and best I could. It sure didn't ease the pain, but it got me closer to Bolivian people and Bolivian society.

I enrolled at the Catholic University and audited courses on the history of Bolivia, culture, and politics. I had made no mention that I was a priest, neither to the family with whom I lived nor to the students at the university. I wanted to be accepted on my own terms, as just a regular person with no title or distinction. But their curiosity about this gringo in their midst gradually uncovered who I was and why I was there.

A group of students at the university organized a project to reach out to the desperately poor who lived on the streets of La Paz and slept under bridges of the polluted Choqueyapu river that flows through the city. The students asked me to celebrate a Mass for these street people. I accepted, of course. But then wondered what in the world I would say to those desperately poor people, who probably had little hope of even eating that evening, let alone gaining the attention of almighty God for their plight. What words of hope or encouragement could I possibly say to them, that wouldn't be just some pious preaching.

I searched the Gospels. In so much of scripture, Jesus seems to be talking to the ruling classes and calling them to repentance, to care for the poor in their midst, to change their hypocritical attitudes. Where does he talk directly to the poor? I found it in his Sermon on the Mount, where he says," Blessed are you poor, for yours is the kingdom of heaven. Blessed are you who mourn and weep now, for you will be comforted." I tried to preach on that, saying that Jesus showed such compassion for the poor during his life. And he died a poor man, persecuted by society, and abandoned by most of his friends. But he never gave up hope that God was with him.

I don't know if my paltry words had any effect on them, or even our efforts to supply them with some food. There are so many factors that contribute to the tragedy of the lives of poor people, so many factors way beyond their control. Unfortunately, they are caught up in a vicious circle of poverty, which most of them will hand on to their children as an inheritance.

My Future Ministry?

Wondering about my future in this convoluted country, I asked a Spanish priest, who was active in social justice and very knowledgeable about the country, how I should pattern my future ministry. He told me to stay for a couple of years to understand the poverty, the injustices, and the role of foreign countries in exploiting Bolivia. Then go back to the United States and educate your own people about the situation in Bolivia. That wasn't exactly what I had wanted to hear. I planned on spending the rest of my life in Bolivia, although I still had no idea how that would transpire.

My professor of political science at the university was Alfonso Camacho. He was a member of a progressive political party. A year later, after a right-wing military coup took place in the country, he was arrested for his political views and imprisoned in the Coati concentration camp on a little island in Lake Titicaca. One day the prisoners were playing soccer with the guards. They overpowered them, got the few boats on the island and made for shore. The boats were too few so the prisoners had to take turns in the icy waters until they reached shore. From there, they ran overland some ten miles, crossing the Peruvian boarder, and ironically ended up in a Maryknoll parish in Yunguyo. I met Alfonso in Lima a year later and he told me the story of their escape. After the dictatorship, he returned to Bolivia and became the minister of education and, in later years, the governor of Cochabamba.

For the second semester, I enrolled at the state university of San Andrés. It was a much more radical university at the time. Most of the students considered themselves Marxists and revolutionaries. They did not think kindly of the US nor of gringos in their midst. So when fellow students asked me if I was from the States, I usually replied, no, I was from Canada. Until one day someone asked me how many provinces there were in Canada, and I stuttered and stammered to avoid giving an answer that I did not know.

The president of Bolivia in 1970 was Alfredo Ovando Candía, a military general who had taken over the country in a bloodless coup. Initially his government was progressive but in the face of conflicts and with pressure from the military command, his government became more repressive of the workers, peasants, and students who continually demonstrated for greater justice in society.

Néstor Paz

A young ex-seminarian, Néstor Paz, appeared in the jungles leading a guerrilla band with the pretension of picking up where Che Guevara had left off in 1968 and starting a national revolutionary movement. He died of starvation in the Yungas jungle a few months later and his movement dispersed. But he was considered a hero by other young people, someone who would give up his life for his ideals and the dream of really changing society. He justified his taking up of arms by saying that he and his group were merely trying to defend the poor against the repressive forces of the military and government, which were beholden to the ruling classes. He cited the revolutionary movements for independence started by Simón Bolivar in Latin America against the repressive dominance of the Spanish rule.

In the university, one of my professors was Jaime Paz, the older brother of Néstor. He also had been in the seminary and studied theology. But then he left, went to Belgium to study, and returned to teach Marxism at the university. In one of his lectures, before his brother died, he ridiculed Christianity as an "opium of the people" and an obstacle to motivating people to undertake the courageous struggle for liberation. But after the death of his brother, he again spoke of Christianity, and said that if it could motivate his brother to sacrifice his life, well then, maybe it could motivate others in a revolutionary way. Jaime was also exiled under

Néstor Paz (top) and his "guerrilla journal," *My Life for My Friends*.

La Paz, Bolivia 49

the Banzer military dictatorship a year later.

In 1980, after the dictatorship, he returned to Bolivia, this time to run for president. During the campaign, his plane mysteriously crashed and burned. The occupants were all killed, except for Jaime, who miraculously escaped. He ended up in Sloan Kettering hospital in Washington, DC, with severe burns on his hands and face. I happened to be in Washington at the time and when I learned of his treatment, I went to visit him. I didn't know if the hospital would let me see him, but they did. And I didn't know if he would remember me or want to see me. He was sitting up in a chair, his hands bandaged and his face covered with some kind of greasy treatment. It had only been about a week since the accident. He obviously was still in a lot of pain and discomfort. I told him I was that gringo in his class ten years ago at the university. He remembered, asked how I was doing and if I was still in Bolivia. In spite of all his discomfort, he still made the effort to accommodate me.

He returned to Bolivia after his recovery and went on to win the presidency a couple of times, sharing power one of those terms with his rival Colonel Banzer, who it is rumored was the one who planted the bomb in the plane to kill him.

Once as president, he was interviewed in the US on the "60 Minutes" television program by Mike Wallace. Mike asked him about the role of the US in Bolivia. Jaime replied that Bolivia couldn't do anything without the consent of the US ambassador. Mike pressed him and said, "For example, if you want to nominate someone to your cabinet that the US doesn't like or approve of, could you do that?" And Jaime replied on nationwide television, which later got back to Bolivia, that no, he could not. When that interview was seen in Bolivia, Jaime was severely criticized for admitting publicly the dependency of the Bolivian government on US policies. His Left Revolutionary Movement political party has remained in politics to this day, but bargained away any revolutionary spirit in an effort to share in political power.

Another Coup

During my semester at the university, another coup took place in 1970 and another military general, Juan José Torres, took over power. He was a short, mustached man and much more revolutionary than Ovando. Once in power, he proposed abolishing congress and replacing it with a people's assembly, with representatives designated according to the percentage of the population they represented. That would mean that the working class and rural farmers would have the great majority of representatives, unlike the congress, which was made up of representatives of the elites from the ruling classes and traditional political parties. That did not set well with the small ruling class in Bolivia who reaped tremendous benefits from corrupt political friends. So Colonel Hugo Banzer, with a wink from Richard Nixon, staged a counter coup. This time it was bloody.

Juan José Torres

Colonel Banzer Takes Power

I HAD FINISHED MY YEAR AT THE UNIVERSITY and was working in the inner city parish of San Pedro. On August 20, 1971, we heard on the radio that popular organizations were calling for a popular uprising, for people to take up arms and defend the government of Juan José Torres. From our second-story window at the parish house we could see people crossing the plaza in front of the Church with guns in hand. That was really scary. It was a Saturday afternoon, and soon the shooting started. We knew that people were shooting at one another. Sirens wailed into the night as the shooting continued. The radio talked of many people killed and wounded, and requested help from the Red Cross to rescue the wounded. Father Mauricio Lefebvre, an Oblate of Mary Immaculate priest from Canada, who had been teaching at the university, responded. But he was fired upon and killed. Some say they targeted him because of his revolutionary views.

The next morning, during Sunday Mass, a plane dive-bombed close overhead and strafed the university five blocks away with gunfire to root out all of the revolutionary students who had sought refuge there.

In the afternoon, some young people from our youth group came to the parish and said that the body of Rafael, the president of our youth group, was seen at the morgue. Could we contact his uncle, with whom he lived, and recover the body. We located the uncle and with him drove to the morgue. Inside, scores of bodies were lying everywhere on the ground, all covered with dirt and blood. It was the most gruesome scene I had ever witnessed, and surely dashed any romanticized notions I had about revolutions.

We finally found the body of Rafael. The uncle wailed and struck the body and yelled at him, saying, "I told you not to leave the house. I told you. I told you...." We picked up the body from the dirt and put it into the back of our pickup truck and drove to the parish, where his friends cleaned the body and laid it out for the wake. Another body was brought in, that of an unidentified man whom nobody had claimed. So we waked him too. We held the funeral the following day, amidst the funerals of so many others killed in the fighting the night before.

Thus began the cruel reign of terror under the dictatorship of Colonel Hugo Banzer, surely one of the darkest and most brutal periods in Bolivian history. Juan José Torres escaped to Argentina, where he was later assassinated, presumably by hired guns of Banzer. The politics swung way to the right, as Colonel Banzer began a witch-hunt for all suspected revolutionaries and "communist sympathizers." If they did not flee to another country, they were hunted down, arrested, tortured to divulge names, and often killed. Even those suspect were persecuted. And thus the attack on the convent where I worked in Achacachi.

The Church under Attack

The Church came under specific attack. The progressive stand for the poor of many clergy and religious was attacked as naively sympathizing with communism. Convents and parishes were forcibly searched. Often the government would plant communist literature or even weapons as evidence of revolutionaries in the Church. A climate of fear and suspicion, as I imagined existed in Nazi Germany, enveloped the country. The military, much like the Gestapo, perpetrated fear as a tactic to intimidate people and silence criticism.

After writing to my folks of the bloody coup and the dismal prospects for the future, I received a reply. Mom's letters came with a note scratched on the outside of the envelope. It was barely legible so I ignored it for the moment. The letter inside had various words underlined in red ink. Only then did I begin to realize that they were opening my mail and scrutinizing it for anything they thought "subversive." The scribbled note on the outside of the envelope said, "Nothing of importance here." Bolivian friends told me that was just a warning to not write anything incriminating about the government.

Bolivia's upper classes felt that the Church and its bishops were betraying them by siding with the poor.

A fishing buddy of mine, Fr. Ray Herman from Dubuque, Iowa, was assassinated in 1974, in the little mountain village of Morochata, near Cochabamba. He had been organizing the local farmers into a cooperative to avoid exploitation by rich merchants who never paid a fair price to the farmers for their potatoes. That kind of organizing of the poor was considered subversive. The assassin was finally apprehended but mysteriously escaped from jail and was never heard from again.

The government announced that everyone with any guns or munitions should turn them in, either to the government itself or to other institutions that could act as intermediaries. One day, when we came back from a clergy meeting, our cook said that a man had left a package at the door and told her to be very careful with it and to call the police. We opened the package and found some unmarked cans and other objects that surely looked suspicious. So we called the police. When they examined the contents, they yelled at us to clear out of the building. There were enough explosives in the package to blow up the whole block.

An important undercover military adviser to the Banzer

government in its persecution of subversives was Klaus Barbie. Barbie had been an officer of the Gestapo in Vichy, France, during World War II. Hitler decorated him for his assiduous work in tracking down and killing Jews and others during the Nazi occupation of France, where he was known as the "Butcher of Lyon." At the end of the Second World War he fled to the United States. As a reward for his collaboration with the CIA in giving information about Russia, he was given a false passport with the name Klaus Altman and disappeared to Bolivia. In 1983 he himself was finally tracked down and deported to France, where he stood trial for genocide and crimes against humanity. He died in jail in France several years later, while serving a life sentence.

Cocaine Production

Cocaine production became a lucrative business in Bolivia during the government of Colonel Banzer, and the Banzer family bought into the narcotics trade. He owned extensive land in the Santa Cruz area, which became a processing plant for producing cocaine. Several years later, a well-known botanist who happened to venture onto that secret area was shot and killed. His assassins were never discovered.

During the Reagan presidency (1981–1989), Colonel Oliver North snuck into Bolivia and bought up huge amounts of cocaine from the Banzer family. Drug dealing was a secret way to make a lot of quick money, which was needed to supply arms to the Contras in Nicaragua, who were fighting to overthrow the left-leaning Sandinista government. In 1986, President Reagan and Attorney

Bolivian woman selling coca in an outdoor market in Cochabamba.

Colonel Banzer Takes Power

General Edwin Meese admitted, in the Iran–Contra affair, that profits from secret arms sales to Iran had also been diverted to the Nicaraguan rebels.

Bolivia is actually the third largest cocaine producing country after Colombia and Peru. Cocaine is made from the coca leaf, which is grown extensively in Bolivia. The coca leaf is also a traditional crop grown and used in its raw and benign state by the Indian population to ward off cold or fatigue.

With the rise in cocaine use in the United States, the US government began to tie its foreign aid to Bolivia, as well as Peru and Colombia, to eradication of the coca plant, believing that less production in South America would mean less use in the United States. But eradication met tremendous resistance in Bolivia because of the traditional use of the coca leaf by all Indians. Also the Bolivian government claimed that if all the coca plants were eradicated and the drug traffic defeated, who would supplant the $1 billion dollars that the drug trade brought into the economy every year. In fact, "Coca" Cola originally used coca leaves to give a little lift to their drink. The US government still allows a significant amount of coca leaves to be exported to the States to be used by Coke, with the claim that it is refined to include nothing that could be considered cocaine.

■

Liberation Theology

AT THE TIME that Colonel Banzer began his corrupt and repressive regime in Bolivia in 1971, a Peruvian priest by the name of Gustavo Gutiérrez wrote a revolutionary book entitled *A Theology of Liberation*. In the book, he expanded on the bishops' statements from the Medellín Conference. As a scripture scholar, he showed how Jesus sided with the poor and sought their liberation, building a whole new approach to theology for the oppressed people of Latin America.

I had the opportunity to travel to Lima a year later, to participate in a summer theology course on Liberation Theology offered by Fr. Gutiérrez and others. Summer in Lima is a great time of year. Lima is right on the ocean. And summer is balmy and sunny. Everyone goes to the beaches. Yet when I walked into the hall at the university, it was literally packed with about a thousand young people who were sacrificing their beach time to hear Gustavo Gutiérrez talk theology.

The speaker called us to order and introduced Fr. Gutiérrez. Out came this little man in a black cassock, looking to be around fifty years old. He took his place behind the podium, which almost ob-

Theologian Fr. Gustavo Gutiérrez, author of *A Theology of Liberation*.

scured him. He said, "We are here to talk about Jesus. Jesus came to free the poor. He came to subvert the established order of society which oppresses the poor and to cause a spiritual and social revolution." Well, if we were back in Bolivia, he would have been gunned down on the spot.

He went on to talk about the first sermon of Jesus: "The Spirit of the Lord has sent me to bring good news to the poor, to proclaim liberty to captives, to set the downtrodden free" (Lk. 4:18). He also cited the Magnificat, the prayer of Mary when she visited her cousin, Elizabeth (Isabel). She prayed: "The Almighty has looked upon the humble condition of His servant. His strong arm ruins the plans of the proud. He removes the powerful from their thrones and puts the humble in their places. He fills the hungry with good things and sends the rich away empty" (Lk. 2:51–53).

He told us that the scriptures have too long been in the exclusive hands of scholars and the clergy. The scriptures were written by poor people for poor people. It is now time for the poor to interpret scriptures from their own point of view. And if we want to understand the scriptures, we must join with the poor in their understanding of what Jesus said and did.

The course went on for a full month, with the active participation of students, clergy, and religious from all over Latin America. Later, the Vatican got wind of Liberation Theology and came down hard on its theologians as "communist sympathizers" or proponents of Marxism for talking so much about the problems of the poor. But they could not pin anything on Fr. Gutiérrez. He was a scripture scholar and all of his theology was based on sound theological principles.

■

Achacachi Mission

AFTER A YEAR IN LA PAZ, I yearned to get deeper into the indigenous cultures of Bolivia and immerse myself as a missionary in a totally different culture. I asked to be assigned to the Maryknoll rural parish in Achacachi, in the midst of the Aymará Indians. I hoped to identify with them, to become friends with them, to in some way share their struggles for a more dignified life, following in the footsteps of Jesus.

Before moving to Achacachi, I realized that I needed to study some Aymará language. So back I went to Cochabamba to the Maryknoll language school. In my first class the teacher gave me one of the old-style reel-to-reel tape recorders and told me sit down with the recorder, listen to the tape she gave me, and try to repeat what I was hearing. I knew that Aymará was a complicated, non-western language dating back three thousand years with guttural clicks and other strange sounds. I hadn't really heard much of the language spoken so the tape sounded pretty strange to me. After about ten minutes of trying to repeat what I heard, the teacher returned and told me that I was listening to the tape backwards.

It took me three months to complete the first book, after which I headed for my new assignment. Arriving in Aymará land, I soon realized that I still could not understand anything the locals were saying, let alone speak a sentence in Aymará. Fortunately, most of the men spoke Spanish as their second language; but none of the women did. The women were like

Achacachi is located about three hours northwest from La Paz, in the area known as the Altiplano, a flat strip of land between the eastern and western ranges of the Andes at an altitude of 12,000 feet.

phantoms to me, whispering to one another, but never conversing with me. After returning to language school for four more months, the language started to come. One day I ventured to speak to the phantom women. They lit up, replied, and became persons to me for the first time.

Achacachi is located about three hours from La Paz, in the area known as the Altiplano, a flat strip of land between the eastern and western ranges of the Andes at an altitude of 12,000 feet. The air is thin and the breathing difficult. The temperature never gets above sixty degrees and the nights often get below freezing. There is no heating in the homes. The saving grace of this wind-swept, arid land is the majestic snow-covered mountains.

Five miles to the north of Achacachi is Illampú, reaching up to an awesome 23,000 feet. Two miles to the south of Achacachi is Lake Titicaca, eighty-five miles long with frigid crystal-clear waters. Thirty miles away is the town of Tiwanaku, where spectacular ruins mark the capital of the Aymará empire, which extended from Chile to Colombia and lasted from 500 B.C. until A.D. 1000, much before the Inca empire.

The Aymará people, who still number around two million, inhabit the area around Lake Titicaca in both Bolivia and Peru. They maintain their own language, religion, culture, customs, and social structures. They are a fiercely independent people, clinging to their own ways and suspicious of outsiders, who have generally exploited them since the time of the

Lake Titicaca and Mount Illampú. Achacaci is visible in the middle right. Note the man fishing in a reed boat (left).

conquest.

Together with the Aymará, Bolivia is also populated by the Quechua indigenous peoples who number about three million and are the remnant of the great Inca empire that lasted from 1300 until the conquest in 1533. Their capital was in Cuzco, Peru. Together, these two indigenous groups make up 70 percent of the population of Bolivia, which makes Bolivia the country with the greatest percentage of indigenous peoples in Latin America. (I will later marry Rebeca, whose mother was Quechua and whose first language was Quechua.)

Rural Indigenous Peoples Bear the Brunt of Poverty

The rural indigenous peoples, scattered in small isolated villages throughout the mountain areas, bear the brunt of poverty in Bolivia. Among them infant mortality is almost 50 percent, meaning that a mother must face the fact that half of her children will die before they reach five years of age. Their income is measured not on a weekly or monthly basis, but according to how much money they earn in a year, and that comes out to be about $200. Their houses are bare bones, often having nothing manufactured in them except maybe a tin plate and a tin spoon. Everything else is homemade. No refrigerator, no stove, no sink, no toilets, no television. Obviously, their lives are extremely frugal, but they survive, as they have learned to do over the past couple of thousand years.

A Visit from Dad and Mom

After a couple of years, my dad and mom visited me in my mission. On Sunday I presented them to the congregation. They stood on either side of me before the Mass, looking over the crowd of Aymará Indians before them. As I told the congregation that they had come from the United States to visit us, a few old women shuffled up the center aisle, approached my mother, extended their arms around her and gave her a big hug. Mom could hardly contain herself. They spoke to her in Aymará. Mom asked me what they were saying. "They are telling you how much they appreciate you giving up your son to come and be their priest in Achacachi. They have sons in military service who are stationed far away in other parts of Bolivia and they miss them terribly."

The next day, we traveled out to a rural Aymará village, where we were welcomed cordially. They rolled out their *aguayos*, a kind of colored blanket, on the ground and invited us to sit down. Then they rolled out more *aguayos* in front of us and began spreading out food, the *chuño*, freeze-dried potatoes, *oka*, a kind of sweet potato, some tiny fried fish called *ispis*, a variety of regular potatoes, a few pieces of meat, and of course the *jallpa wayk'a* hot sauce. We feasted, as my folks gazed about them in amazement at being in this faraway place in a strange culture, yet welcomed as family by these enchanting people.

■

Class Conflicts

AFTER ONLY TWO MONTHS IN THE PARISH, the attack on the convent took place. The townspeople began suspecting us of being "communists" or revolutionaries or foreigners opposed to the government of Colonel Hugo Banzer. And it became very difficult to work with them or even relate to them. The townspeople were a class of people distinct from the rural Aymará Indians. They considered themselves more white, more civilized. They were the landed gentry and the campesinos were their virtual slaves until the 1952 revolution in Bolivia. At that time, the townspeople lost their lands to the rural Indian peasants and fled to Achacachi for refuge.

Most of the townspeople also did not like the changes taking place in the Catholic Church in Latin America They were used to their priest responding to their every whim, paying for their baptisms, marriages, and Masses and having them celebrated whenever they wanted. We, on the other hand, required participation in Church activities and an instructional preparation to receive the sacraments. But the townspeople felt themselves above that. We found the rural peasants, the campesinos, very interested in learning, wanting to participate in Church activities, and even assuming responsibilities for ministering in the Church. As a result, we spent most of our time with the campesinos, much to the chagrin of the townspeople.

One day during one of the town fiestas, where a lot of drinking takes place, a neighbor, Señor Mejía, came up to me and said, "Father, you know what your problem is? You bring all these Indians into our Church, and make them your leaders. They were our slaves up until a few years ago. We will never receive Holy Communion from their hands. We will never listen to their sermons in Church. We'll never receive religious instructions from them. And we won't let our babies be baptized by them either."

These townspeople prided themselves on being descendants from the Spanish. Since the time of the conquest of Latin America in the 1500s until the 1952 revolution, the descendants of the Spaniards, the oligarchy or aristocracy, owned all the land, and forced the indigenous population to work their lands, giving them a small part of the harvest. Properties were bought and sold with the Indian workers included. Some of the elderly campesinos told me they remembered the days when they were whipped if they were caught with a book or tried to learn to read or write.

An example of the Bolivian oligarchy was a man by the name of Simon Patiño. In the 1920s and 1930s, he was actually one of the richest men in the world. He made all his money in Bolivian mining. Minerals have always been one of the greatest natural resources for Bolivia.

Silver Mining

Shortly after the conquest, the Spaniards discovered what was to become the richest mountain in the world: Potosí. During the colonial times, Spain extracted enough silver from that single mountain to build a bridge to Spain. Upon its discovery, Potosí became known and famous the world over. Thousands of Spaniards flocked to Potosí and it became the largest city in the Americas during the late 1500s and early 1600s. It is not an attractive place to live. The altitude is 15,000 feet. The climate is cold. The land poor, wind-blown, barren, and without vegetation. The silver was plentiful and transported by llama herds up over the Andes and down to the Pacific coast, where it was shipped to Spain. There the riches were squandered by the royalty on meaningless wars and lavish living. Pirates raided the ships at sea and further

Cerro Rico, Potosí, Bolivia.
At the height of Spain's exploitation of Potosí's enormous reserves of silver, "hundreds of campesinos died in that awful mountain every day. Today Potosí is one of the poorest cities in Bolivia."

wasted the minerals mined at a tremendous price in human suffering.

The Spaniards brought in Black slaves from Africa, but the cold, altitude, and forced labor decimated them. The Spaniards then instituted a system known as the *mita* in which all of the Indian villages had to send a percentage of their able-bodied men to Potosí every year to work in the mines. Most of them died. At the height of Potosí exploitation, hundreds of campesinos died in that awful mountain every day. They were forced underground for months at a time. They ate and slept underground. Those that emerged were often blinded by the light of day. Hundreds of thousands of Blacks and Indians were sacrificed in the extraction of silver for Spain during that period.

Now Potosí is one of the poorest cities in Bolivia. It can still boast of lovely colonial churches built by the Spaniards and the Catholic Church, to attend to the wealthy pious Catholics who saw no contradiction in praying to Jesus and decimating the poor Indians. They sucked all the wealth from that mountain, squandered it in lavish living, and when it was over, left poor Potosí high and dry, almost a ghost town, just a shadow of what it had been.

Rebeca, my wife, is from Potosí. She experienced firsthand the poverty of that once opulent city.

Simon Patiño followed in the footsteps of those Spanish exploiters. How could anyone make millions and millions of dollars in Bolivia? It could only have happened by using cheap labor and accumulating most of the wealth for himself personally. He built a lavish mansion in Cochabamba, Los Portales, but because of poor health, he retired to France and never lived in it.

Revolution of 1952

All of this changed dramatically, though not definitively, in the revolution of 1952. The workers and Indians were getting educated and more aware of the inequalities in Bolivia. They were ripe for revolt. The National Revolutionary Movement (MNR) rallied them to throw off the yoke of exploitation and install a new, revolutionary government. Many lives were lost and the cost in human suffering was dear. As a result, the private mining interests were nationalized and the wealthy landowners driven off their estates. They fled into the cities and towns, like Achacachi. They still harbor bitter memories of those days long past and hate the Indians for it.

Religious Conflicts

AS A NEW MISSIONARY in the radically different Aymará culture, I fell into the trap of criticizing the local religious practices. I actually felt it my responsibility to correct some practices that I thought were pagan or not in keeping with our Christian faith.

One such experience was the All Saints Day celebration, which is one of the major religious feasts in Bolivia and for the Aymará. The local custom is for those who have lost a family member during the past three years to set up a table altar in their home. They decorate it with bread figurines called *t'anta wawas*. These are figurines of people, of animals, of a ladder to climb up to heaven, of angels, of stars, the moon, the sun, etc. The table should also contain all the foods that the deceased person liked to eat, including some drink, like the native corn brew *chicha* or a small glass of alcohol.

Traditional Beliefs

The traditional belief is that at noon on All Saints Day, the souls return. So people go to the cemetery to receive them and usher them back to their homes. Then they invite all their friends in on the eve of All Souls Day to say some prayers, receive some refreshments and accompany the soul of the deceased. The following day, after a night of visiting, praying, eating, and drinking, the soul is accompanied back to the cemetery, where the family again wants to send the soul off in good stead. So they take food and drink to the cemetery and have a little picnic at the gravesite.

I thought this was all a little superstitious, and a big waste of money for poor people. So I preached against it at the All Souls Day Mass, saying that the souls are happy in heaven, do not come back to visit us, and do not need our food.

In the parish, a young man, Julio Rojas, had gone off to the seminary to study for the priesthood. He was one of the first Aymará Indians to do so and we were very proud of him. Julio had come back to Achacachi to gain a year's experience with us before his ordination. He heard my sermon and got quite upset. He told me that I did not understand nor appreciate the culture and religious beliefs of the people. "We have a deep devotion to our deceased relatives." he told me. "We believe they are very close to us and not far away. We can relate to them, and they to us. We want them to be happy, and this is the way we express those beliefs and sentiments." I realized that my own mother told me that she often talks to my dad, who had passed away years ago. She said she feels that he is very near to her.

Years later, the dear brother of my wife was killed suddenly in an automobile accident. On the following All Souls Day we set up an altar in our home, with all the foods that he liked and invited in our friends to pray for him. It was a very sacred and solemn moment for us and one that we repeated for three years.

People would always come to the parish and ask for a blessing of the deceased before taking the body to the cemetery for burial. On one such occasion, the people had been drinking quite heavily all night at the wake in their home. After the blessing at the parish, the pall bearers lifted the casket up on their shoulders to carry it to the cemetery. But the two in the front were facing in the opposite direction of the two in the back. They tugged amidst muffled giggles from the onlookers. Realizing their dilemma they put the casket down, and lifted it again, only to realize that they all turned around, and were now facing each other. Others more sober joined in and eventually carried the casket away to the cemetery.

My first Christmas was also a cultural shock to me.

Christmas is not one of the main religious feasts in the Aymará culture. It is just another minor feast day, when the Indians come into town for market day. But there is no commercial anxiety around Christmas as in the States. The only distinctive feature is the Sheep's Mass. And that is exactly what it is.

I walked into the Christmas Day Mass and was greeted by hundreds of sheep filling the pews, together with their little shepherd boys and girls. I really did not appreciate the scene but went ahead and celebrated the Mass, to the accompaniment of plenty of baaahs. After the Mass, I asked one of our religious leaders why they bring all their sheep in for the Mass. The Mass is supposed to be for people to worship and celebrate their faith. I was a little disappointed to see only sheep and shepherd children at the main Christmas Day Mass. He reminded me that God revealed the birth of Jesus first to a group of shepherds who were tending their sheep. When they went to worship the Christ Child, they surely took their sheep with them. And for this particular day, he said, we also want to bring our sheep to share in the worship of the Christ Child.

On Sundays, after the Masses, people would gather to have their babies baptized. Often there were twenty to twenty-five baptisms at a time. I would line up the mothers with their babies in arms in a circle, and have their godparents stand behind them. One woman stood alone, and I asked her if she was the mother or the godmother. Often the parents would send in another person to baptize their child. She insisted that she was the mother, pulling out her breast and showing me that she had milk for nursing her child. That was shocking to me, but for the Aymará, breast feeding in public is common practice.

My earliest attempts to transmit information to our religious leaders in workshops were a total flop. Our categories and ideas of knowledge, understanding, science, and religious doctrine clash with their concerns to simply experience reality, to celebrate reality, to feel and participate in what they perceive around them.

Pacha Mama
Mother of All Things on Mother Earth

In one of my first workshops, I thought it would be a good exercise to help them distinguish the good and bad spirits in their culture, and also in our Christian faith. So I asked them to name some of them. They began with the Pacha Mama, the mother of all things on Mother Earth. "Well, obviously she comes from God and is good so we will put her over here in the good category," I said. They protested, "Wait a minute. She can sometimes be a little nasty, and we often have to placate her with offerings so she will grant us good crops." So I said, "Well okay, how about the *supay*, your devil spirit? Surely he goes over here in the bad category." Again they protested that sometimes we can also deal with him, and he can avoid some bad luck for us. "Well then let's get back to our faith and put God in the category of all good," I insisted. "Not always," they contested. "Sometimes He can also be nasty, like in the Old Testament when there were wars, or He punishes people for their sins." I was getting nowhere with them, and began to realize that my western cultural categories were not adequate to understand their culture or mentality.

Then thinking that they needed some help in organizing a sermon, I gave a course on developing their ideas for preaching. I told them that they needed a strong beginning, develop the theme, and finish with a practical application. Well, they couldn't get it. They continued to preach round and round, repeating the same ideas over and over again. Even our good deacon, Julio Rojas, followed the same pattern. Later I began to realize that my mind was programmed in a linear fashion from proposition to conclusion. Their Aymará perspective was, on the other hand, much more cyclical, repeating and reinforcing the same ideas in various ways. I had much to learn about teaching them. I needed to let go of my ways of thinking and judging and accept a whole different reality if I wanted to at all be in touch with the Aymará culture.

Capturing the Spirit of Faith

One of the best religious leaders of the parish was Néstor Escobar. He was a shy Aymará Indian man, soft-spoken, but could look right through you with his big black eyes. He became one of the best preachers at the Sunday Masses. But he always came to church looking like he had just finished plowing an acre of land with his team of oxen. I asked him once about that, and suggested he try to dress up a little for when he would preach at the Sunday Mass. He responded, "It doesn't make any difference what I look like on the outside, but what my inside looks like and how that gets conveyed to the people in what I say."

He had captured the spirit of faith from many religious courses in the parish, but he still lacked a few details about Catholic liturgical practices. On one occasion I observed Néstor giving Holy Communion to little children. After, I told him that Communion was reserved for older children and adults who had completed instructions in First Communion classes. He replied, "Well, I only gave them a little piece. I couldn't turn them away."

One Sunday, while giving out Holy Communion, I too was confronted with a little boy standing on the sidelines, observing the people sticking out their tongues to receive the host. Then he got in line, approached me, and similarly stuck out his tongue. I held up the host and asked him what it was. He just looked at me, not having figured out that part. A minute later he was back in line. This time he said, "God." No, you still don't have it. This is the Body of Jesus. You have to get some instructions from your catechist before you can receive Holy Communion.

Communal Celebration

Later, I came to realize that Holy Communion has a whole different meaning in the Aymará culture. For western society, it is more of an individual devotion, to receive the Body of Christ into my body. For the Aymará, it is more of a communal action, a part of the ritual that the whole congregation shares in. There are no individual devotions.

For Holy Week, leading up to Easter, I told all the catechists to gather together the people in each of their villages and read the Bible with them. Explain to them about the last days of Jesus, the Last Supper, his arrest, his crucifixion on the cross, and then his resurrection. The following week we had a meeting of all the catechists of the parish and I asked them what they had done in their villages with their people to celebrate those solemn days. Rosendo told me that the people of his village of Taramaya gathered together on Thursday to celebrate the Last Supper. He said that they sang some songs and prayed and then told him that he should take the part of Jesus. They brought in some bread and soda, and he read from the Bible how Jesus took them and said that they were his body and blood. Then he distributed them to all the people gathered and everyone shared the bread and soda, in memory of Jesus. Hmm…I wonder if that was an actual Eucharist celebration?

One Sunday, I asked Juan Canaviri to read the Gospel and preach at the main Mass in the Church. He was a relatively new catechist and had never done that before. He approached the podium, opened his Aymará Bible, and began to read. I tried to follow in my Aymará Bible but couldn't locate what he was reading. And then he preached, and again I had difficulty following his train of thought. After, I asked Juan to show me what he read. He fumbled around with his Bible until finally I pointed out the Gospel he was supposed to have read. I asked him to read it to me. He couldn't. He didn't know how to read. He had faked reading and preached on just a lot of scattered ideas, not wanting to lose face with me or the congregation.

Creative Interpretations of the Bible

On another occasion in the village of Awichaca, the people gathered for a celebration, and acted out the parable of the Prodigal Son, as related by Jesus in the Bible. A young man addressed his father and mother, though the mother is not in the Bible version. He asked for his inheritance to leave home. The parents got into a big argument, again not in the Bible, about whether to give him his inheritance or not. Finally, they agreed and off the lad went. He squandered his money and ended up feeding pigs, and the people of the village brought in a bunch of real pigs for him to feed. Finally, he repented and went back home, where his parents received him. The Aymará campesinos are very creative, free and concrete in interpreting the Bible according to their own reality.

Like my friend Néstor. At a Mass on the feast of the Assumption of the Virgin Mary, I asked Néstor to read a section of the Book of Revelation. There St. John describes a dream about a woman giving birth, but a dragon waits to devour the child, a reference to the cruel authorities at the time persecuting the Church of Jesus. Néstor added his own version that the child got scared and retreated back into his mother's womb with the dragon after him. And they had a big fight within the mother's womb. I asked Néstor where he got that idea. It was certainly not in the Bible text.

While visiting the village of K'asamaya, two old women asked if they could go to confession. Their little Church was locked, but they said we could just talk in their house. The two of them sat down on a couple of sacks of potatoes and began relating little incidents in their lives, correcting one another as they went along. They were lovely, candid, and seemed to genuinely enjoy the opportunity to chat with me about the ups and down of their past lives. That was their confession.

After several months in the parish, one of the catechists asked me to become the godfather, the *padrino* to his child. I was flattered and considered it a great honor, feeling that maybe I was becoming accepted into their culture. After the baptism, they invited me to their home for the *rutucha*, which I knew nothing about. Rutucha is a hair-cutting ceremony, an Aymará initiation rite for small children. My godchild, somewhat bewildered by all the attention, was seated on a table in the middle of the small adobe house. Relatives and friends gathered around him. First the parents and then the padrino approached the child, were handed a pair of scissors, and offered a lock of the long hair that had not been cut until that moment. The snipped lock of hair was then deposited in an *aguayo*, a colorful Indian weaving, where the cutter was also expected to deposit some money for the child's future. Then the cutter drank a hefty bowl of *chicha*, the Indian brew, and was offered some coca leaves to chew, a necessary element at all Andean rituals. At the end, the child was pretty much bald, with some added snipping by the padrino to even up the first haircut. Then they counted up the money and advised me that I had to make up the difference for the money to come out to some 100 peso number. The *aguayo* with the locks of hair and money were carefully wrapped up and saved by the parents. In the Aymará Altiplano, a calf or lamb might also be offered for the child to raise, after a spraying with a shaken bottle of beer for good luck. The rutucha is not to be missed, as important in Andean society as baptism. Our own children have been no exception.

In Achacachi, which was becoming something of a mystical reality to me, a man by the name of Patricio wandered the streets, with a plastic bag over his head, lugging a few belongings in a tattered bag. I tried to speak to him one day, but he only smiled a silly smile and looked away. The following Sunday, as I entered the empty church to prepare for Mass, I heard Patricio chanting near the altar. I stood in awe at the beautiful prayer he sang over and over again, kneeling alone in the church. In a sermon, I mentioned the incredible example of that humble devotion of Patricio.

■

Cultural Conflicts

ONE SUNDAY MORNING, I went to the plaza to buy some eggs for breakfast. An elderly Aymará woman sitting on the ground had several eggs on a blanket spread out before her. I asked her to sell me a dozen. She said, "*Camisaki, Wirajocha,*" which means, "How are you, worthy stranger?" I asked her again to sell me a dozen eggs, but she said no, she couldn't sell me that many. "But you have more than a dozen here," I replied. She looked at me quizzically and said, "Well, if I sell all of them to you, what will I do all day?" So I chatted with her a few minutes and bought four eggs, anxious to get back home for some breakfast.

Later I thought about that little incident, and realized the world of cultural differences between myself raised in western society and this ancient woman, steeped in her Aymará culture. I had approached her for a strictly economic deal, her being an autonomous seller and myself as an autonomous customer. I presumed there would be a set price and I would pay her the money, take my product and leave. She, on the other hand, considered our encounter quite differently. She was sitting in the plaza with some eggs, which for her were like charms to attract people to come sit with her for a while and chat. She was not interested in making a lot of quick money for herself. What I considered a purely economic transaction, in the Aymará reality was more of a communal and social exchange, without personal interests.

A woman came to the door one day and asked me to accompany her to find the spirit of her son. Apparently he had been frightened by a dog, and had been out of sorts ever since. The Aymara believe that in cases like this, the spirit of the person may remain in the place where he or she was frightened and had to be called back. She took me to the place and produced a bundle of clothes wrapped to look like the child. She began ringing a bell and called the child by name. Then she beat a strap on the ground and told the spirit to go back home. This may seem quite strange to us, but don't we also say that someone is out of sorts? Or that they had the wits scared out of them? Or that someone is not him/herself today? Well, if they are not themselves, who are they? The Aymara believe full well in those unconscious insinuations of ours and concretize them in a ritual to bring the spirit back to the person. Now when our children are sick and out of sorts and nothing seems to help, my wife often repeats the same ritual.

Investigating a Death

Rumor had it that a man had been killed in the chapel of one of the villages. Their annual fiesta was coming up, and the village asked for a visit and a Mass to celebrate their fiesta. Some of the catechists from the area encouraged me to look into the killing first. When I visited the village, the leaders told me the victim had come into the village and stole someone's belongings and some animals. He was drunk, and when he tried to escape, he fell into a hole and died during the cold night. I thought if he were drunk, he probably wouldn't have frozen to death.

Finally, after some prodding, they admitted to having killed him. This was the third time the same person had come into their village from a neighboring community and stolen from them. Actually, they captured him and dragged him into their little church, the only public building in the village. People were quite angry and began beating him. As the ordeal wore on, some people began drinking, and the beatings got worse. They tied him up and left him over night. In the morning he was dead.

I asked them why they didn't call the police from Achacachi, or drag him into town to be jailed and tried. They told me they did not have confidence in "white justice." The man would have paid a small fine and been released. The village would also have had to pay for the arrest, detainment, and trouble caused to the police. So they took things into their own hands and executed their own justice. Even people in the cities, I was later to learn, do not confide in corrupt police officers and the local judicial system. Thieves captured by neighbors have sometimes been lynched or even doused with gasoline and burned.

Aymará woman and her child.

Not only did the Aymará not trust the outsiders' justice system. They also did not trust the politicians and the whole political system of Bolivia. Talking politics one day with Felix, our catechist, he told me, "It doesn't make any difference whether the government is left or right, conservative or liberal. For us, they are all the same, ignoring the plight of the campesinos and acting for their own interests." That attitude would change dramatically with the election of an Aymará Indian to the presidency in 2005.

Bolivia's Health System

The health system of the country falls under the same dubious pall. The rural Indians of Bolivia fear doctors from the city and hospitals. And well they might. One day I was asked to take a young girl into the hospital in La Paz, since nothing seemed to be helping her in her village. At the hospital, no one spoke Aymará. They began yelling at her in Spanish to take off her dirty clothes and get a good shower. She couldn't understand why they wanted her to disrobe, as the Aymará are very modest. And she had never taken a shower in her life. With fear and confusion she submitted, was treated and returned to her village, but never again to return to a city hospital after such humiliating treatment.

On another occasion in Achacachi, a man fell and broke his leg. I took him to the small clinic in Achacachi, where the doctor told him that it was a compound fracture, and he would have to go to La Paz to have it set with screws. I summoned our ambulance, but his family would not let him get in. They said he would die in La Paz, as so often happened. Well it did happen, because often people waited until the last minute, in desperation, as a last ditch effort, before taking someone to the hospital in La Paz. I argued that the break could be fixed easily. He would be back home in a few days and would be walking normally in a couple of months. Without that treatment, he would be crippled for life. They stubbornly refused to let him get into the ambulance, began shouting at me, and would not let me pass. In my anger and frustration, there was no other option, but to let the family have its way and take him back home. I was not in control of the situation in this strange corner of the world.

Fr. Joe Picardi, who would later join us on our team, was

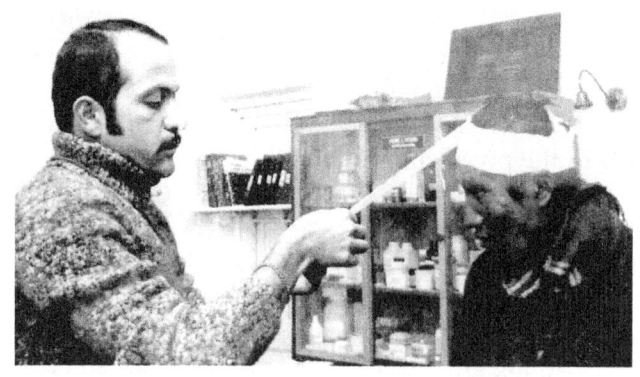

Maryknoll Father Joe Picardi, a nurse,
treating an Aymará patient in the parish clinic.

a nurse, and he gave courses to the local people to prepare them to become barefoot doctors. They would learn basic health care and be able to help people in their isolated villages with some first aid. On a visit to one of those villages, the local health promoter, Felix Choque, asked me to accompany him to visit a sick person. We entered the dark adobe hut and encountered an older man lying on the floor wrapped in blankets. Felix talked to him and then took both his wrists in his hands, to take his pulse. He stood there in silence for a few minutes, and then said he had improved. "How could you take his pulse," I asked Felix, "if you don't have a watch?" "I know. I can tell." he replied. He also told me that he mixed his own serum for giving injections. Now that was something that was not taught by Fr. Joe in the course for health promoters.

Does Prayer Work?

Another day, while visiting the remote mountain village of Murumamani, the catechist asked me bless a blind girl in her home. She was sitting alone in the darkness of her small hut, crying. She said her parents were leaving her to die. The family could not support a child that could not help out with chores for the survival of the family in the harsh and desperate Aymará Indian reality. We prayed, and I wondered if prayer really worked, if miracles could really happen, and if this prayer of ours might actually help her see again. We told her to go to Achacachi and see the doctor. Maybe he could do something. She said she was afraid to leave her house. And her parents fatalistically doubted anything could be done for her. So I volunteered to take her, convincing her family that they could come too and we would be back in the village later in the day. The doctor examined her and gave her some drops to improve her vision. Unfortunately, I wasn't able to follow up with her, and don't know if the medicine actually helped her to regain some sight…and live.

Loneliness

A COUPLE OF MONTHS AFTER THE ATTACK on the convent in 1971, the conservative priest with whom I had been working left for the States on vacation and never came back. With the Sisters exiled, I ended up alone in Achacachi for the next six months. Those were lonely times. I liked the adventure of immersing myself in the Andean Indian culture. But I was always an outsider. It takes a long time to become a friend of the Aymará people. They are suspicious of outsiders and only after months or years of respectful friendship does one gain their confidence. During the days, I was on the road with my motorcycle to visit one of the sixty-five rural villages and our religious leaders. But back home at night, I would huddle alone around my kerosene stove to keep warm. This lonely existence was not my cup of tea.

I wondered whether anyone cared that I was in Achacachi. What difference did it make that I was out there on a lonely mission post in the middle of nowhere, struggling to keep warm and keep my spirits up? I thought of so many others in comfortable surroundings with friends close at hand.

One day I drove my motorcycle up the mountain road, through Warizata to the side of the Illampú mountain. I drove off the road close to the 17,000 foot permanent snow line and parked as close to the sheer steepness of the mountain side as possible. Majestic Illampú rose 6,000 feet almost straight up in front of me. But between us dropped a deep

Majestic Mount Illampú

chasm. I was so small, insignificant, vulnerable. There was no one but me, and the spirits of the mountains. I shivered as the cold wind howled around me, and I felt overwhelmed at the grandeur of the immense mountain in front of me. It was desolate, quiet, bleak, and I became frightened. I felt an urge to leap. What was that urge to destruction? I felt like Christ being tempted in the desert, alone and facing terror. I had wanted to come to this edge to test myself, to test the Lord, to face God alone and without all the security I usually had around me. I prayed a desperate prayer and slowly backed away from the edge. Trembling, I mounted my motorcycle and retreated from the temptation of that awful beauty.

Rather desperately, I talked with the priests in the neighboring parishes of Peñas and Huarina, who also were alone. And we decided to form a team, live in one central place, Achacachi, and from there serve the other parishes.

■

New Start

AT LAST I HAD SOME COMPANY and some people to share ministry with: Jake Esselborn, Bill Allen, John H. Moran, and John Turner. Jake would later transfer to Bangladesh to take on a new mission for a few years, then had a heart attack playing handball and passed away. John Moran went to Bangladesh with Jake but later left Maryknoll and married the sister of my friend Bill Lafferty. Bill Allen married Eduarda, the Bolivian Sister who had been involved in the convent incident in Achacachi. And John Turner returned to the States and married a woman in Miami. Three Maryknoll Sisters, Margaret Smith, Joan Mury, and Teresa Gleason, also joined us on the team, with a warning from the bishop that the men and women not live under the same roof.

Later, Gene Toland, fresh from the States, Joe Towle, having been thrown out of Guatemala, and newly ordained Joe Picardi, a nurse, joined our team.

Paul and Fr. Jake Esselborn, 1975

Formation of Aymará Leaders

MY NEW COMPANIONS collaborated in the formation of religious leaders in Achacachi, both men and women, in most of the sixty-five outlying Indian villages. Cirilo Willca, Santos Appease, Néstor Escobar, Felix Choque, and Encarnación Huanca were our principal religious leaders. The five of them oversaw different sections of the parish and taught in various courses.

Every month we had a general meeting with all the religious leaders of the parish and over one hundred and fifty Aymará Indian men and women would trudge over the mountains from their villages, sometimes three hours each way, to come for that gathering. They enjoyed the stimulation of learning and being part of a unique dynamic movement among the campesinos throughout the area. We offered more extensive courses to them in leadership, literacy, the Bible, history, and health. They would take off five days from their farm duties to participate in a course. Neighbors in their villages would often pitch in and help take care of their fields or animals.

In one of the courses we explained to them the "Universal Declaration of Human Rights" from the United Nations. The document spoke of the rights to assembly, education, a decent job and income, a fair trial, and to be treated with respect. Participants in our courses had never experienced these rights in the course of their history and especially not now, during the time of the Banzer dictatorship. They asked me when the document was written. "In 1948," I said. "What!!" they cried out. "Why have you hidden this from us for so long?"

Learning to Teach Bolivian History

We also gave a course on Bolivian history. To illustrate the period of the conquest of Latin America by the Spaniards, Gene Toland and I dressed up like the conquerors. He put on a helmet and carried a sword. I wore a cassock or priestly gown and carried a Bible. We didn't tell them what was coming. We just walked into the classroom and began shoving them into a corner, taking the desks from them. We spoke in English and showed them a fork and, told them to use it to eat with. I showed them the Bible and pointed up to God. Out of respect for us, they did not react. But then, we stopped and read a passage from the Medellín bishops conference about the injustices of the conquest. And we told them to talk about that statement among themselves.

We went out for a few minutes, and then came back, repeating the same abusive treatment. But this time the catechists did react, and started to push back and resist us. They got the message about the conquest of Latin America by the Spaniards. That sad page of history resulted in the decimation of the Indian populations of North, Central, and South America. When Columbus arrived the indigenous population was estimated at eighty million. One hundred and fifty years later, the indigenous population of the Americas was only eight mil-

Fr. Gene Toland using hand puppets as props during an educational program in Acacachi, Bolivia.

lion. Seventy-two million indigenous people had been exterminated either by new germs or by slaughter.

In the Latin American Bible, there is an excellent introduction that explains the history of the

Paul and Fr. Gene Toland, 1975

world from the creation account on into the sacred history portrayed in the Bible. We decided to explain this section in one of our courses to the religious leaders. But we realized that our western history is linear. It has a starting point at creation and an ending point at the present. Whereas their concept of time is circular. It starts one year at the preparation of the land for planting and ends the next year at harvest time. And then repeats itself. So if we wanted to introduce a linear time scheme, we needed to expand their horizons.

We started by drawing a line on the blackboard, indicating the present year. Then we worked backwards, asking them the year that they were born. They dug in their pockets and pulled out their identity cards and checked the dates. Birthdays are not noteworthy events in the Aymará culture. We indicated the years on the line as we extended it backwards, to 1955 and 1945. Then we asked them when their parents were born. They had no idea, but they were like fifty and sixty years old. So at the time they would have been born in the early 1900s.

We asked them when Bolivia had a war with Paraguay and then with Chile. Some of their parents or relatives fought in the Chico War with Paraguay in the 1930s. And some of them recalled the war with Chile when Bolivia lost its seacoast, the end of the nineteenth century. So we marked those on the horizontal line, extending back in time. I asked them when Bolivia won its independence from Spain, and with a little prodding, someone recalled Independence Day as 1825.

Another mark on the line. And when did the Spaniards arrive in Latin America? When did Pizarro conquer the Incas and begin the conquest of the Incas? That was way back on our line to 1533.

Then I asked them, what happened before then? They replied, "Well, I guess there was just us here." We marked the Inca empire back to 1300 and then the Aymará empire, more extensive than the Incas, reaching way back on our line to the other side of the room to 500 years before the birth of Christ. Wow! They never imagined that the Aymarás had an empire that stretched back over fifteen hundred years.

I asked them if they had ever studied their own history in school. And they said no. They learned some history of Bolivia and the colonial period. But never anything about their own history. In the teachers' college some mention was made of Inca and Aymará history. I felt embarrassed that I, a foreigner, was teaching them something about their own history. On our time line, the Aymará and Inca empires occupied half the room, over two thousand years. And the colonial period from the conquest to the present was only five hundred years. Then we came back to the present, and they asked, "What happens now?" "Well," I said, "that depends on you."

Religious Congregation of Aymará Indian Missionaries

One of the Bolivian Sisters working with us, Mary Figueiredo, took a keen interest in forming the young Aymará women of the parish. Eventually, they formed a Religious Congregation of Aymará Indian missionaries. They maintained their own traditional dress and sought to maintain a close identification with their own people. The movement thrived and grew and over the years some fifty young women would associate with these Aymará missionaries and travel to isolated villages to spread the Word of God.

Marriage Rites

WE ALSO HAD COURSES to prepare young Aymará couples for marriage. Their parents wanted them to get married in Church, and we saw that as an opportunity to invite them to come to Achacachi for a course for five days. I remember greeting one of the young girls at the course, about sixteen years old, in the Aymará language. She didn't respond. Rather, she had a glazed, distant look in her eyes and wouldn't look at me. She seemed completely bewildered. I asked one of our Aymará religious leaders why she wouldn't respond. And she said that for many of them it was the first time out of their villages. And they were scared. The girls in those isolated, primitive villages, would awake in the morning, help prepare some food for breakfast, take the sheep or llamas out to graze in the mountain passes, return in the afternoon, help prepare some food for supper and go to bed. There was very little stimulation in their lives. It was routine, quiet, and extremely simple. But coming into Achacachi, they experienced for the first time an interaction with other young people, talk, questions, music, dancing and sports. Toward the end of the course, they would get into it, and began to open up and participate in the activities.

On Sunday, during the Aymará Mass, I would marry them, sometimes as many as fifteen couples all together. They would line up around the altar and I would go to each couple, performing the Catholic marriage rite. One couple I did not recognize, and they did not have any registration papers with the parish. I asked them, and they said they didn't know they had to inscribe beforehand. I told them I couldn't marry them. They pleaded, saying everyone was waiting for a big celebration after Mass. So we made a deal. I would stop in front of them but not perform the ceremony, giving the impression to the congregation that they were getting married. But they would have to return the following week, inscribe in the parish books and receive some instruction in the faith. They agreed, had their celebration afterwards, and returned the following week for the details.

My Western Ways

In my western ways, I always thought that one of the roles of a priest was marriage counseling. I waited for three years and no one ever came. Finally one day, one of our Aymará religious leaders, Santos Appease, asked me to talk to a couple from his village who were having difficulties in their marriage. I welcomed the opportunity, and he said they would be back in the afternoon.

Santos returned with the couple and fifteen other people. I asked him who they were and what was happening. He said they were the parents, the aunts and uncles, the godparents and the leaders of the village. They always participate in such discussions, but they wanted me to be included. The couple sat on the floor and we all sat on chairs in a circle around them. The leader of the village asked the man what his problem was. He said his wife was dirty, didn't cook for him, didn't take care of the animals, and was always complaining. Then he asked the woman what her problem was. She said that her husband was mean to her, was lazy, drank too much, and didn't provide for the family.

The leader then told them to be quiet. He began to scold them, telling them how irresponsible they both were, how they were causing problems not only for each other but also for their families and the whole village. They had to stop fighting, start working and taking care of each other, stop drinking, start cooking. They were married now and there was no going back. Then the next person started in and rebuked them in the same way, and so it went all around the circle, until it came back to me. They asked, "Well, what do you have to say, Father?" I joined the choir and told them they had to get back together, to stop fighting, to start taking care of each other.

The leader of the village said that we had to give them the punishment for stepping out of line and causing so much problem for the village. "We whip them," he said, and gave me the whip. Whoa, I protested. "I have never done this before. Couldn't someone else do it?" So the village leader took the whip and ordered the couple to kneel down on the floor, and remove their heavy jackets. He told us all to leave the room. In my curiosity, I peeked back through the door and saw him wind up that whip and crack it over them, hitting the floor more than the couple. He repeated that a few times and then invited us all back inside. The couple sat down, someone brought in some crackers and soda and we celebrated that the couple was repentant and now back together. They had hardly anything to say about it! I asked our religious leader what would have happened if the couple refused to collaborate. He said that they would have been banned from the village, losing their land and all their inheritance. They would have had to go off to the city and try to find a new life, without the help of family or friends. So they conformed.

That would never happen in western society where we have such a strong sense of individuality. Marriage is a personal thing, and people resent anyone butting into our private lives. We rebel at anyone who tries to force us to conform. But these people live in a radically different situation. They live on the edge, do not have a lot of margin of safety for their survival, and need to depend on one another. They cannot tolerate people doing their own thing or stepping out of bounds. They demand conformity to the community norms. That seems to us like a restriction of freedom, and I suppose it is. But it is the price that is paid for belonging. And the benefit is the support and collaboration of the rest of the community.

Aymará Cosmology

AN OUTSIDER WOULD SAY that the Aymará people are superstitious. They have many, many spirits and believe that everything has a spiritual dimension. They see either evil or good spirits in everything and every event. These spirits must be dealt with in a positive way, placated, or else they can cause you a great deal of harm. A strange rock or clump of earth can be a bad omen. Worse is to come across a toad or some bones. A lightning bolt is a very powerful sign from the spirits. It can destroy a house or animal or person on the high, barren Altiplano. If a person is struck by lightning and survives, he or she becomes a *Yatiri* in Aymará, one who knows, a shaman, medicine man, or holy person in the village. They would be called upon to deal with the spirits and to seek remedies for whatever seemed to be the problem, whether a sickness, accident, crop failure, or some other instance of bad luck. There are also people in the Aymará culture who deal with the occult, "black magic," casting spells and using evil forces to cause harm to people. I don't understand all the workings of these various "spirits," both good and bad, but I certainly respect them and prefer not to mess with them.

Every Thursday, at the top of the Surucachi hill outside of Achacachi, the Yatiris would gather and be available for consultations with the people. An anthropologist from Denmark, Lizbeth Overgaard, was staying with us for several months to help us understand the Aymará culture. She wanted to go up the hill one Thursday to observe what they were doing. I told her that I would take her, but not to observe. The Yatiris would never permit that. But if she wanted to go up and consult them, that would be fine. So she inquired around to find out what she needed to bring. She gathered together a small woven cloth, some coca leaves, which are considered sacred, and some alcohol to sprinkle on them.

Consulting a Yatiri

We joined the line of people waiting to consult one of the Yatiris. When our turn came, we sat down on the ground in front of him, surrounded by several Aymará women who were curious to hear what these two outsiders were going to say. Actually, they were very helpful. They told us how to spread out the cloth on the ground and arrange the coca leaves on it. The Yatiri asked us what we wanted to consult him about. Lizbeth, the anthropologist, said she was worried about her grandmother, who was quite sick. The Yatiri took a handful of coca leaves and raised them in the air. Then he let them fall back onto the cloth. He did this a few times, and began to sort through them until he found a certain leaf. He raised the leaf and said that was the grandmother. The leaf was somewhat wilted at one end and slightly damaged at the other. He said that the grandmother was having trouble with her head and her feet. But the leaf was basically sound, and the grandmother would recover. Going back down the hill to town, Lizbeth told me that her grandmother was getting senile, and had recently fallen and broke her leg. And that was the concern that she brought to the Yatiri.

Lizbeth was not a Christian, and one day she asked me

"El Yatiri," oil on canvas by Arturo Borda (1883–1953).
If a person is struck by lightning and survives, he or she becomes a "Yatiri" in Aymará, one who knows, a shaman, medicine man, or holy person in the village.

what was God's plan. We always seemed to be talking about God's plan. Was it explained in the Bible? What a great question. I fumbled around for a while, and finally remembered what Jesus had said: That all may be one. And St. Paul said: The great mysterious project of God is that everyone may be united. Unity among all His people is the great plan of God. And anything that causes division or conflict is obviously against God's plan.

The Aymará people believe that an unbaptized baby that died would bring terrible bad luck to the village. So when a village suffered some catastrophe, like a drought or hail or blight on their crops, they would look around the village for a young girl who may have been pregnant but did not now have a baby, believing that she had had an abortion. Often they would find someone, and come to me for a blessing of the fetus or the girl or the village.

People would also call on me when they encountered something strange, like some carved rocks or bones, and ask me to come and bless them. Actually, in that way I discovered a lot of ancient ruins, stone carvings, and even skeletons from several hundred years ago. In the village of Umacha, people asked me to bless some skulls they unearthed. The skulls were elongated, a custom for royalty in the prehistoric times of the Aymará empire. Apparently they would wrap something around the back part of the skull of small babies to make the skull stick out as a sign of special privilege in their culture.

The Andean peoples have an innate religious sense about them, based on a belief that everything is sacred and needs to be related harmoniously with everything else, including humans. That's why when the Spaniards arrived in South America, and preached adherence to the Catholic religion, the Andean peoples said, "Sure, why not. These people probably have some pretty strong spirits. And maybe those spirits can help us too." So they baptized their babies and got married in Church and went to Mass. But then they would go back home and practice their own rituals too. They were covering all the bases.

The most profound religious sense that I found in the Andean culture was a sense of awe for all of nature and God's creation, and a need to live in harmony with creation. We in western society seem to have lost that sense of awe of nature. We live in a society where we think we pretty much control everything. We live far from nature, and most of our surroundings are manufactured. The immensity and mystery of nature are far away, unless we take a camping trip, go fishing or go hiking for a few hours, and are somewhat stirred by the great outdoors. But these people live daily very close to nature, and treat it with great respect. They believe that everything is connected, and do not separate their religion from other aspects of their lives. Everything they do has a spiritual dimension and must take into consideration the effect on everything else. Nothing is isolated, which translates into a sense of unity and solidarity among themselves. No act is performed that does not have consequences on other aspects of their lives. They realize deeply that they do not control their surroundings, rather they are dependent on something or someone far beyond themselves. They intrinsically honor and are humbly beholden to that something or someone, without an explicit explanation of who or what.

Their principal spirits are Mother Earth, called Pacha Mama or the Mother of all things, and the sun, called Tata Inti, Father Sun. They pray upward to the sun

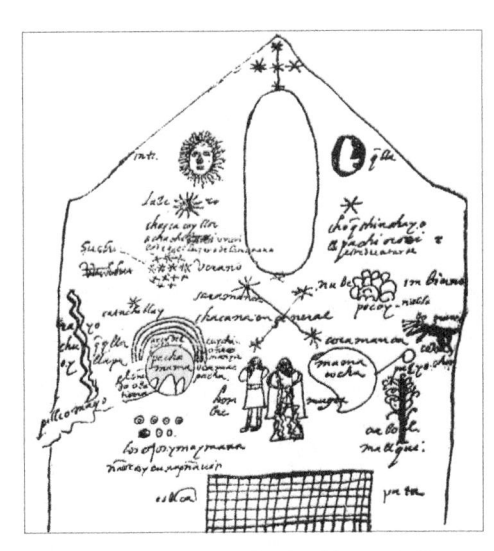

Representation of Pacha Mama in the cosmology illustrated by Juan de Santa Cruz Pachacuti Yamqui Salcamaygua (1613), after a picture in the

Aymará Cosmology

and downward to the earth. Whenever they drink anything, they always pour a little bit first on the ground, as an offering to Mother Earth. When they plant, they always bury an offering in the ground first, made up of candy, colored wool, small amulets of people or animals or different plants. Also included are little tablets with symbols of bounty, like a good harvest. They say that in ancient times, it was wrong to plow with a steel blade. It was too harsh on Mother Earth. It was better to just use a wooden plow, pulled behind a team of oxen. Wood grew out of the earth and was less alien and harsh than manufactured steel.

The Dancing Black Llama in the Sky

Astronomy is a hobby of mine. People had mentioned to me that there is the figure of a huge black llama dancing across the sky, and it can only be seen in the high Altiplano on a dark night. Late one evening, I glanced up in the sky and was overwhelmed by the myriad of stars, so many that the brightest stars of constellations were almost lost in the background of millions of other stars. But there were dark areas of the sky, splotches where hardly any stars could be distinguished. People had told me to look for the dark eye of the llama in the constella-

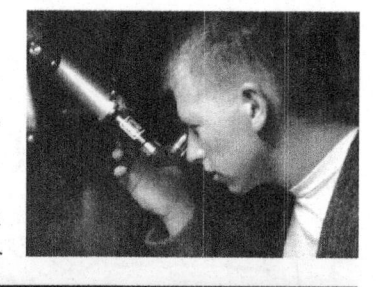

One evening Paul was once able to spot the "Coalsack Nebula": an arrangement of stars in the form of a black llama stretching halfway across the sky, down from the eye of the llama through the Milky Way, its body extending into Scorpius and its feet dancing across Sagittarius.

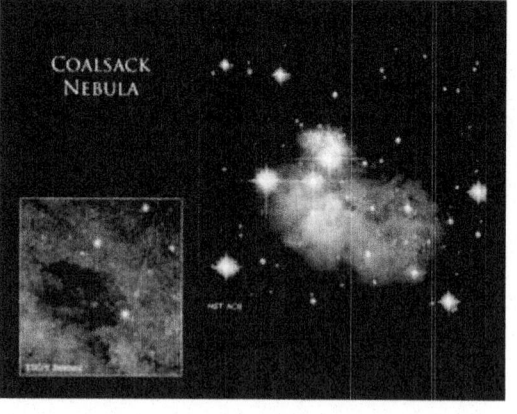

COALSACK NEBULA

94   *Pilgrimage*

tion of the Southern Cross. In astronomy books, this dark patch is referred to as the Coalsack Nebula. Suddenly I was awestruck as I saw the whole black llama, stretching halfway across the night sky, down from the eye of the llama through the Milky Way, its body extending into Scorpius and its feet dancing across Sagittarius. I sometimes was able to point out this phenomena to Bolivian friends, who were completely unaware of this breathtaking sight in their night sky.

Close by Achacachi towered a mountain sacred to the Aymarás called Pachjiri. Few outsiders seemed to know about it, except the local Indian people. My seminarian friend from Achacachi, Julio Rojas, took me up the mountain shortly after I arrived in Achacachi, and showed me the various sacred places venerated by pilgrims to placate their spirits. It was an awesome place, with an incredible view of the snow-capped mountains to one side and the blue waters of huge Lake Titicaca to the other. The flat plains of the Altiplano, dotted with villages and farms, stretched before us. It was quite understandable why this place held such mystical meaning for the local people.

Years later, I asked Néstor to take me up the mountain again, but this time in August, when hundreds of local people with their village Yatiri would ascend the mountain. They believed that August was a special month. In the southern hemisphere, it is the beginning of a new agricultural year. It is the end of winter, and a blustery month of transition. People believe that the spirits are stirred up by the winds, and it is not a good month for significant events, like marriages or baptisms. What transpires during that month has an awesome significance for the rest of the year.

We climbed a couple thousand feet up the rocky slopes. Néstor warned me that the people would be suspicious of me, an outsider, a gringo, intruding into their sacred space. It may even be dangerous for me, as they may drive me off the mountain. The people were curious, but many of them recognized me as the town priest. They certainly wondered why I was there. I tried to be as unassuming as possible and stay in the background of all their activities, knowing full well that I was being offered a rare glimpse into the very private and mysterious world of the ancient Aymará.

Two huge stones pointed upward and Néstor explained that this was the place where the new Yatiris were consecrated. At the very top of the mountain, a group of people were gathered with their Yatiri. He grouped them together and wound a ball of yarn around them, like tying them up. Then his demeanor changed and he angrily ripped the yarn off them, threw it on the ground, spit on it, and cursed it. Néstor explained that he was freeing the people from their sins and all evil that bound them. The Yatiri then told them to take off their jackets and sweaters, reverse them and put them on again, as a symbol of new life.

Ritualism Not Dogmatism

The Aymará are very ritualistic people in their religion, but not very dogmatic. They have very little dogma to explain why they do things or the significance of their spirits. They are more interested in celebrating the mystery of their surroundings, which brings them in more direct contact with those mysteries, rather than trying to figure them out. In seminary we were taught to respect other world religions, like Buddhism, Judaism, Hinduism, Islam, and other ancient religious traditions. And here I was being confronted by the ancient Andean religion, not well known in theology books nor well understood.

Once in a course, I asked our catechists if God was among them before the Spaniards arrived. They at first balked and mentioned that the Spaniards brought the Word of God to them. Then they considered it, and quite boldly said, "Well sure, God was here long before the Spaniards. He was always with us." Then I asked what He was doing among them. They reflected and said, "Well, He was guiding our people. He was inspiring our people. He was accompanying our people."

■

Outsiders

OFTEN WHEN I WAS FILLING UP MY MOTORCYCLE with gas, the townspeople would ask me where I was going. I would tell them, to visit the village of Parqui Pararani or the Rinconada, way up in the mountains. They would tell me to be careful because it was dangerous up there. Often people who are running away from the law hide out in the mountains. And the Indians up there do not like outsiders. They eat people.

What? I asked some of our catechists about that, and they told me the story. Shortly after the 1952 revolution, one of the landowners continually returned to his ex-hacienda and required the Indians to pay him a tribute of potatoes and wheat. He would often be accompanied by a military or police officer. But one day, during the fiesta in that village, the man returned alone. The people had been drinking and were angry to see him. They started to attack him and eventually killed him. And to further vent their anger, they burned him, and even ate some of the remains. That's why when people mention Achacachi, they say they eat people there. But I never had any problem going into any village.

The only time it came close to danger was once when I traveled way up into the mountains to visit a small, remote village that no priest had ever visited. By that time, I was getting pretty good in the Aymará language, and could converse fairly well with the people. We were going to celebrate a Mass, but it was getting toward late afternoon, and the catechists of the area who had accompanied me, warned me that I'd better leave because the people still do not have confidence in you, and if night falls, you might be in danger. They might push your pickup into the mountain lake. So I gracefully thanked them for receiving me, encouraged them to participate in Church activities, and took my leave.

Denouncing Abuses

Several of our religious leaders began complaining to me that ex-landowners were coming back to their villages and pressuring them to give them some of their harvests, as they had been forced to do before the revolution of 1952. I decided to talk to the authorities in La Paz and put a stop to this abuse. So one day I went to the office of the minister of agriculture, Colonel Alberto Natusch Busch, who later became president in a bloody coup in 1979. His secretaries asked me what I wanted. I told them that I was the priest from Achacachi, and had some information that I wanted to share with him about the campesinos in the area. I waited a short while and they escorted me into the minister's office. He was cordial and seemed genuinely interested. He asked me for the information, names, places, and dates. I had it all documented and gave him the information, which his secretary copied in full. Satisfied, I returned to Achacachi, naively believing that the military would effect some justice, the local police and military detachment in Achacachi would be warned to not accompany ex-landowners to the villages, and the abuses would stop.

On the contrary, a week later, the campesinos from those villages came in and asked me what I had done. I proudly told them that I had denounced the abuses directly to the minister of agriculture. They told me that everyone on the list had been summoned into the Ministry and criticized for giving that information to me. They were now scared that they would be further persecuted and their villages would have many more problems now with the military and local authorities. I really stuck my foot in my mouth, trying to do some good and achieve some justice for the campesinos. But I learned that I shouldn't do things on my own like that, without consulting with the campesinos beforehand. They were the vulnerable ones and they had much more experience and knowledge of the complicated and dangerous game of political affairs.

Facing the Archbishop

One day, I received notice from the archbishop of La Paz, Monseñor Jorge Manrique, to come to his office to answer some questions about my pastoral work in Achacachi. He showed me a document denouncing my pastoral work, with the signatures and rubber seals of over thirty authorities from Achacachi. I didn't think there were even that many authorities in town. They included the mayor, the military captain, the police chief, the sub-governor, store owners, and teachers, among others. They criticized me for not granting them the sacraments of marriage and baptism, for not being available in the parish house, for not celebrating Masses that they wanted, for letting unworthy people run Church programs, etc., etc. They demanded that I be replaced.

The archbishop asked me what I thought of the criticisms. I explained that the townspeople were not at all collaborative with the Church, they wanted the Mass, baptisms, and marriages without any instructions, wanted special favors, and did not show any interest in having their own religious leaders trained. Generally, they just wanted some rituals and sacraments to fulfill cultural obligations, without any commitment to participate in formation programs to mature their faith. On the other hand, the campesinos participated very actively in the Church and had over one hundred of their own religious leaders who were eager to study the Bible and learn more about their faith. So most of our time was dedicated to the campesinos.

The archbishop understood perfectly. He asked me what we should do. I told him that it would be very difficult for me to return to my pastoral work in Achacachi under the present denouncement. In fact, the annual town festival was coming up in a week, and a series of Masses was always a part of the

Paul conducting a religious service in Achacachi, Bolivia.

festivities. These would be very difficult for me to fulfill. He suggested a retraction. I agreed. And said that if all the people that signed the denouncement would sign a retraction with the same signatures and seals, I would be willing to continue on in Achacachi. He wrote a letter to them stating that option, and saying that the Church in Achacachi would be locked until he received the retraction.

I took the letter back to Achacachi and of course, the big shots were infuriated. They wanted those Masses said for their fiesta, and said there wasn't time in a week to collect all those signatures again. I told them that it was out of my hands. The mayor, who was a young upstart and a drunkard, appointed by the dictatorial government of Colonel Banzer, said he would blow off the doors of the Church with dynamite. Well, they finally came through with all the signatures, and I celebrated the Masses, though not with great enthusiasm. After the Mass, the drinking started. A fight ensued at one of the parties and a military guy who was drunk took out his revolver and shot and killed the person with whom he was fighting. But as would be expected, he was simply transferred to another town and never prosecuted.

■

Winding Down

AS TIME WORE ON, I WORE OUT. After six years in Achacachi, I began to lose my enthusiasm for this great adventure. I was getting cranky and short-tempered with the people and wondered if maybe I was doing more harm than good by staying there. One of the first Maryknoll priests, who went to China and later became a bishop, wrote: "A missionary goes to a place where he is not wanted but needed, and stays until he is wanted but no longer needed." It seemed that our programs were well on their way. Many catechists and religious leaders had been formed and enthusiastically embraced a faith commitment to Jesus. I felt satisfied that I had given Achacachi my best shot and some of the best years of my life.

I talked with my religious superiors and they suggested I return to the United States for a while and work promoting our Maryknoll missionary work. But I felt like I was giving up the ship, abandoning my mission work and my people. I looked around at the other Maryknoll priests who had been in Bolivia for twenty or thirty years and were still at their posts. I bet they came down to Bolivia like me with a lot of piss and vinegar, all enthusiastic about serving the Lord and the people. But then, after many years of loneliness and frustrations, trying to give themselves to the people, and getting so little back, they burned out. But they stayed at their posts. They came down to Bolivia as missionaries to give their lives to the people, and by God, they would do it. They would die with their boots on. They would not admit defeat or throw in the towel. So they stayed. But often they became bitter, resentful, lonely old men. A few thrived and maintained a lively, loving, open spirit. But they were few. Bolivia is like that. It eats people.

Saying Good-bye

So I decided to end up this phase of my mission career and go back to the States for a while. Who knows. Maybe those feelings of worthlessness, of purposelessness, of futility, would pass by some day, and not last forever. Maybe I could recover my enthusiasm. Maybe even come back to Bolivia.

I began to say good-bye to my hard-won friends in Achacachi. The Aymará campesinos surprised me. They always seemed to be rather quiet, unemotional, and stoic people. The cold, harsh weather in the Altiplano seemed to have created that character. But when I told them I was going to be leaving, many of them got very emotional and cried, even the men.

They invited me out to a village high in the mountains for a meeting, with the pretense that it would be one of our last monthly catechist meetings in the villages. But it turned out to be a reception for me. The village was tucked in a little green valley, surrounded by towering, snow-capped mountains, among quaint thatched-roof huts. It all seemed like a Shangri-La. About twenty-five of our religious leaders from that part of the parish had gathered. Their wives were busy someplace out of sight. We

Paul was honored to be given a red pancho by his parishioners.

102 *Pilgrimage*

men had our little business meeting, and then the women came out with flowers. They had woven a beautiful garland, which they placed on my head, and another, which they placed around my neck. Some musicians appeared and began playing jovial Andean melodies on their panpipes, which are so typical of the ancient Aymará folklore. And we danced, joining hands in one big circle. Afterwards they brought out the food that they had cooked for the occasion, simple but with an outpouring of hospitality. I couldn't believe the joyfulness of those mountain people. And I couldn't believe that I was there in their midst, reveling in their warmth and affection. This was truly a unique experience for me. My heart filled with emotions and I joined them in laughing and crying tears of joy. As I look back on that experience, it almost seems unreal, maybe just imagined. But I remember returning to the parish in the late afternoon with the flowers still around my neck and sharing that overwhelming experience with my coworkers.

Spending Quality Time: Our Pastoral Style

The week before I was to leave, the religious leaders of the parish organized a festival in my honor. Several native musical groups performed for the crowd that had gathered. In one of the testimonies, Felix Choque praised me for coming out to their villages and eating with them. I thought that was just a routine part of our ministry. But later, Julio Rojas told me that priests who ministered in the parish before us would take their sandwiches and soda out to the villages when they visited and sit in their jeep and eat alone. And then they would quickly scoot back to the relative comfort of the parish house in Achacachi. As a pastoral team, we had decided from the start to spend quality time in the villages after celebrating Mass and told the people we wanted to eat with them.

At one of our courses in evangelization, representative catechists from all the parishes in the area were instructed to draw a picture of the missionaries. One of the most memorable and disturbing pictures drawn by a group of native people was of a jeep speeding away from a village. The group explained that often the missionaries drive out in their jeeps, say Mass, and then speed away. They wanted us to leave our jeeps at home, to walk out to their villages, as they did, and spend time with them, without rushing away.

So we had made a decision as a parish team, in our early years, to make a point of spending a day or two in a particular village, visiting with the people, sharing time with them, which is the biggest commodity they have. We also told them that we were coming out to spend the day and would welcome a gathering of the whole village to celebrate with prayers and a picnic-style meal, which was so typical of their culture. And sure enough, when we arrived we would usually celebrate Mass, which they wanted held in their little chapel. Then we would all go outside and sit down on the ground in a big circle. The women would bring out their brightly colored woven *aguayos* and lay them on the ground in a long line. Then each family would place their contributions of food on the blankets and everyone would pick out what they liked, sit back on the ground, and we would eat together. If I stayed overnight, they always cleaned out the best room in their simple house and gave me the best bed they had. In the chill of the morning, often with temperatures around freezing, we would wash up in a cold mountain stream, and then stand on the side of a building facing the sun to warm up.

Well, those visits to the sixty-five villages in the parish were the fondest memories I had of Achacachi. Apparently, they were for the people too. At the going-away celebration, they presented me with a red pancho. They explained to me that you can't buy a red pancho. It is woven particularly for each leader of the village, as a sign of his authority. These leaders were called *Mallcu*, which also means "condor," the sacred majestic bird of the Andes. And they wanted me to have one of those special ponchos, as a sign of my authority in the Andean culture.

A few days before leaving, Néstor, Felix, Cirilo, and Santos came to the parish. We visited for a while. Then I started getting anxious about all the packing I had to do and all the work I had to do to wind up my ministry of the past six years in the parish. So I excused myself. That evening, they were still there. I asked them if they weren't returning home that evening. They told me that they were staying until I left. It was their custom, to accompany someone who was leaving on a long trip, to cheer them up so they would not be sad. Right up to the end my anxious efforts got in the way of their hospitality and spending quality time in friendship.

Thirty years later, one of our most respected religious leaders from the village of Chijipina Grande, Genaro Clares, came to visit me in Cochabamba. He brought me another red poncho and presented it to me as a token of our friendship and in memory of my years in Achacachi. I asked him if I could wear it, knowing that I was an outsider and the poncho represented a respected authority figure in their culture. He assured me that I could. He told me that most of the religious leaders that we had formed during those days went on to become civil leaders of their villages and of the surrounding area. Many of their children went into the seminary and became the first cadre of Aymará priests in Bolivia. In December of 1976 I wrote the following in my diary: "The people here seem to be discovering a refreshing (though often conflicting) newness about their lives. A people are awakening. I felt a desire from the start to participate with a people in their awakening and discovery of their destinies. And it's happening. It is not just new structures. It is a new realization. The people involved (the campesinos) are not even aware of it."

"...You People Made Me a Woman"

I remembered a similar conversation that I had with Encarnación, the Aymará woman who had been caught in the attack on the convent in Achacachi. Years later I met up with her. She told me that she married an ex-seminarian from a neighboring parish and they had several children. They had asked permission from the bishop of the area to work in a parish as a lay missionary couple. The bishop gave them a very remote and isolated parish in the mountains beyond Achacachi, which had been without any religious attention for many years. She told me that they repeated the same program that we had done in Achacachi, that of training religious leaders in each little village and instructing them in the faith to lead their own people. I was so elated to realize that what we had done in Achacachi was something that they themselves felt was valuable and in harmony with their culture.

Then she blew me away with the following comment. She said, "My parents raised me, but you people made me a woman." I knew I couldn't take all the credit for that. We had been a team, together with several Religious women, who were involved in their formation. But it certainly was gratifying, after so many years, to know that our work had been appreciated and had born fruit in the Aymará culture. So many missionaries never know if what they did ever had any positive affect. As Jesus said, "Some plant and others harvest." All you can do is plant the seeds.

■

Sojourn Back to the USA

AFTER LEAVING ACHACACHI, I asked Maryknoll if I could take a few months off before beginning my new ministry in the States, explaining that I wanted to visit several of our other missions in Latin America. It would give me a wider experience of the various works and places where Maryknollers practiced ministry and a more global view of our work, for preaching in churches. They generously agreed.

The long trek would also actualize something of my spiritual philosophy of life. I believe that we are like pilgrims, on a convoluted, often mysterious path of life. The road is not always clear, nor clearly marked. The traveler must often make the road, with all the risks and apparent dangers. Dead-ends are inevitable, so one must have the humility and courage to return and start over. The adventure draws one deeper into the journey. Hopefully it is not a solitary journey. Hopefully there are fellow travelers along the way who are willing to share experiences gathered, failures suffered, and wisdom learned. I believe it is the only way to find life, fulfillment, meaning, and happiness, and which will finally bring me home to my true self, lived in God.

Also, ridding myself of so many means of support would make me more aware of my radical dependence on God and that without Him, all my pretensions and illusions of security are really only distractions from the life of God within me.

Travels with Roy

At the time, Roy Bourgeois had just been thrown out of Bolivia by the Banzer government dictatorship. During his initial language training in 1972, he had written an editorial letter that was published in several major newspapers in the States, denouncing the US military aid given to the Banzer government, aid that was being used to repress any dissent among the Bolivian people. That did not endear Roy to the Bolivian government.

He had been assigned to work in La Paz, taking a room in a poor neighborhood above the San Pedro parish. There he built a school and clinic for the people. We became fast friends and always got together to share our struggles on my trips into La Paz from Achacachi. He began a ministry of visiting political prisoners, of which there were many, in the San Pedro jail. Again, the government was suspicious of Roy and his involvements. In their distorted view, he was supporting communists. He was arrested in 1977, tortured, and warned that if he continued his involvement with left-wing movements, he might not be harmed, but his people would be. He realized that it was becoming too dangerous to continue his ministry in Bolivia and agreed to leave.

Roy Bourgeois visits a women's cooperative in La Paz, Bolivia.

The Banzer government finally collapsed in 1977 after a long protest begun by poor women from the mining area. The government had arrested their husbands as subversives because of several strikes for better wages and working conditions. They were put in concentration camps or deported out of the country. The women and their families were left without any means of sustenance. A few days before Christmas, seven of them marched into La Paz with their children and began a hunger strike. People tried to convince them that the holidays were not a good time to begin a protest. But they were determined, and soon thousands joined them in hunger strikes in churches around the country. Banzer finally relinquished and called for an interim government and elections. Subsequent governments could not hold the country together and after a brief period of democracy, the military again stepped in to take advantage of the lucrative drug trade and impose a harsh rule on Bolivian society.

I told Roy that I was going to hitchhike back to the States. He said he would join me in Panama and we could travel together through Central America. I calculated that I would be in Panama the Friday before Holy Week and we could try to rendezvous in the airport.

So began my sojourn of three months from Bolivia to Minnesota, by land. I began writing a journal of my spiritual journey.

Leaving Bolivia, I took a bus up over the Andes and down to the coast of northern Chile, wanting first to visit our missions in Chile. On the long bus ride down to Santiago, I felt a euphoria of freedom, to have my ministry in Achacachi and Bolivia behind me. I was no longer a sore thumb in a small town, battling the altitude and cold, coping with a strange culture and defending myself from nasty political accusations. I was free! On my own! Anonymous! The Atacama desert rolled by on one side and the Pacific ocean on the other. I was at peace.

Two days later, I arrived at the Maryknoll headquarters in Santiago. I asked a friend to take me out for some Chilean culture and music. We ended up at a nice restaurant, where a couple of young women sang some songs. My friend, who did not speak very good Spanish and had had a few drinks, was approached by the waiter, who whispered something in his ear. He just said, "Si, Si." I asked him what the waiter said, and he replied that he probably just wanted to bring us another round of drinks. Well, it was the young women who had been singing. They came over, sat down and ordered the most expensive drinks for themselves. We tried to make small talk and then clumsily excused ourselves.

I visited our missions south of Santiago where the Atacama desert turns into fertile green fields like Wisconsin. I took time to ski at Portillo, where the winter Olympics once took place. Then back north to the Maryknoll headquarters in Lima, Peru, continuing north to Quito, Ecuador, where two Maryknoll Sisters hosted me. Leaving Quito, I hitched a ride with four young people driving to Venezuela. The two guys and two girls were anxious to get to Colombia to buy some good marijuana.

In Bogota, we stopped at some friends of theirs for a visit. A young boy, about twelve years old, asked me where I was from and what I was doing. He asked if he could correspond with me when I returned to the States. So I gave him the address of my folks in St. Paul. Back on the road, I made my way to the Maryknoll headquarters in Caracas, Venezuela. Five minutes after arriving, they told me I had a phone call from the States. This was the only reference date and phone number that I had given to my folks for my long trip north. It was my brother, Don. He asked if I was all right. Sure, no problem. He said they had received a letter from Bogota, Colombia, saying that I had been beaten up and was in a hospital. Please send $200 immediately to the enclosed address. That little shit! My folks were worried sick and had frantically tried to contact me through the US embassy in Colombia. But, of course, I was not to be found. Then they remembered the Maryknoll contact in Caracas.

After touring our works in Venezuela, I tried to book a flight to Panama to meet Roy. It was the beginning of Holy Week, and all the flights were full of holiday travelers. I went to the airport early in the morning, begged and tried to bribe a ticket, and finally succeeded on the last flight out of Caracas to Panama. Arriving at the Panama airport, I wondered what I would do now, and where I might meet Roy. Suddenly, I heard someone call, "Hey, Pablo!" It was Roy. He had also just arrived from the States.

■

Central America in Revolution

Nicaragua

WE VISITED SOME MARYKNOLL SISTERS IN PANAMA, traveled up through lovely Costa Rica, and then entered Nicaragua, a police state run by Anastasio Somoza, a wealthy and ruthless dictator, who had been referred to by a US president as "a son of a bitch, but he is our son of a bitch." The Maryknoll missionaries there filled us in on the civil war going on in the country, waged by the Sandinista Front for National Liberation (FSLN) that was seeking to topple the repressive Somoza government.

At the Sisters' house, we met a young man who offered to take us up country to see some of the rural areas. We asked the Sisters if he was trustworthy, and they assured us he was. The next morning he picked Roy and me up and drove us several hours north through Matagalpa, until we were stopped at a military checkpoint. A big soldier with a big gun dressed in camouflage fatigues asked our driver for identification. Then he recognized him and waved us through. Whoa. That was a red flag for us. Was he friends with Somoza's military thugs? Roy had become really paranoid from his recent experience with the military in Bolivia and wanted to turn back. But how would we get back? We didn't even know where we were. We drove on and finally arrived at a rural village that our guide said was our destination. But he had hoped there would be horses there to take us up into the mountains.

"Christ Crucified in Nicaragua,"
by artist José Ignacio Fletes Cruz

Again, Roy said, let's get out of here! This is too dangerous with a civil war going on all around us. But our guide encouraged us on. We walked a couple of hours up a narrow path, through the thick underbrush. Our guide had hurried on ahead of us. We thought, they could ambush us at any moment and no one would know about it, a couple of gringo priests snooping around this politically volatile area. Suddenly we saw our guide far below us, in a clearing, by a little farm house, surrounded by a number of other men. We thought, this is it. They are waiting for us down there. Who are they? What do they want with us? We had no other option but to make our way down to where they awaited us.

Our guide explained that this was a meeting of the religious leaders from the area. They had gathered to prepare for Easter Sunday. This was Saturday, the vigil of Easter. The catechists embraced us and welcomed us and thanked us for making the long journey to be with them for their meeting. They were really flattered that we two priests would come all that way and join them in their preparations. We celebrated the Eucharist with them, and after they related the many atrocities they had suffered at the hands of the Somoza military, who were extremely suspicious of any movements among the poor peasants, and especially Church people who might be talking about human rights or worse yet, liberation.

A few months after our visit, President Somoza ordered the bombing of the Solentiname monastery of Religious Brothers, who were outspoken supporters of the rights of poor peasants.

In 1979, Somoza would be driven from the country by

the Sandinista guerrilla movement, and a Maryknoll priest, Fr. Miguel d'Escoto, would become the foreign minister in the new government.

El Salvador

ON TO EL SALVADOR, a political situation even worse than Nicaragua's. El Salvador had just had elections and masses of people flocked to the central plaza to protest what they considered a rigged election. The government responded with force, sending the military in to disperse the crowds, with live ammunition. Our Maryknoll people in El Salvador told us that it was a bloodbath. After the slaughter, the government sent in trucks to wash the blood from the streets.

This was 1977. A new archbishop had just been elected, Monseñor Óscar Romero. He was considered a conservative, much to the liking of the Salvadoran military who thought he would not make any noise about their brutal repression of dissidents in the country. About the time of our visit, and three weeks after Romero's consecration, his dear friend and fellow priest Fr. Rutilio Grande was gunned down by the military for raising the awareness of the peasants to their God-given rights and dignity. Five other priests would be martyred in 1977 and 1978. These killings sparked the conversion of Archbishop Romero to grasp the plight of the poor and they ignited in him a tremendous courage to speak out against the brutality of the military. Little did they know that they had a cat by the tail, a cat that would not let go. The military finally

Monseñor Óscar Romero with Fr. Rutilio Grande to his left.

killed him a couple of years later.

Roy and I would both return to El Salvador for visits and the atrocities we witnessed would indelibly mark our future lives and work.

Guatemala and Honduras

ROY AND I MOVED ON TO GUATEMALA, which similarly was experiencing a civil war. This time, the conflict was between the military government and the Mayan Indian peasants, who made up the majority of the population. Guatemala had a history of repressive governments, broken only by what was called the ten years of springtime, 1944–1954. But the springtime did not last. The US accused the democratically elected government of Jacobo Árbenz Guzmán of not respecting the wide power the United Fruit Company wielded in that country.

Washington felt Árbenz was too lax with the unions and too soft on communism. President Dwight D. Eisenhower, his secretary of state John Foster Dulles, and the CIA decided Árbenz had to go. They stirred up protests and misinformation and Árbenz was forced to resign—one of the great tragedies of Latin American history, and the beginning of forty years of genocide against the Mayan Indian peasants. More than thirty thousand Indians were massacred in the process.

Roy and I visited with Fr. Ron Hennessey, the Maryknoll superior for Central America. He shared details of the death of Fr. Bill Woods, a Maryknoll priest, whose small plane carrying a group of Indians for resettlement out of danger's way, was shot down in 1976, with no survivors. The Guatemalan military and the US ambassador had warned Bill that his life was in danger. The later cover-up by the military confirmed the suspicion that Bill had been ambushed. Cardinal Mario Casariego y Acevedo, the leading Catholic prelate of Guatemala at the time, was of no help. He only warned other Maryknollers to "stay out of politics." In 1998, however, a Truth Commission of the Catholic Church published four volumes of information on past violations of human rights in Guate-

Maryknoll Father Bill Woods was flying a group of Indians for resettlement out of danger's way in Guatemala when his plane crashed under suspicious circumstances.

mala, 90 percent of them attributed to the military and government death squads. Two days after that report was released, Bishop Juan Girardi, the instigator of the report, had his skull smashed in. The plight of the Indians in Guatemala and the involvement of Fr. Ron Hennessy, are documented in the book *Through a Glass Darkly: The U.S. Holocaust in Central America*, by Thomas R. Melville.

Hunger in Honduras

Roy and I found our next stop, Honduras, to be equally grim, though the country was not experiencing a civil war. Accompanying brother Maryknollers in their ministries to the poor, I saw for the first time in Latin America children suffering severe malnutrition and with bloated stomachs.

■

Minneapolis

AFTER HONDURAS, Roy left me to return to the States. I continued on to Mexico to visit more Maryknoll friends. But since I was so close, I decided against more excursions and took a bus directly back to Minnesota.

Finally I was back home. After a few days, however, I began to feel the itch to get back on the road again. I began to realize that I had left home by one door and had returned through another. It was not the same place anymore. And I was not the same person who had left St. Paul fifteen years earlier. Too much had happened, too many jolting experiences. Home was no longer familiar to me. I felt out of place and began to realized how much I was still living out of the radically different experience I had had in Bolivia among the Aymará Indians, and the horrendous experiences I had just had in Central America. My feelings came out in an irritability I felt toward people around me who didn't seem concerned or sensitive to all the anguish I was feeling for the people in Latin America. My brother Don told me once that he didn't even know what to ask me about, sensing that I was still living in a different world.

Maryknoll was asking me to stay in Minneapolis and promote the works of Maryknoll by raising funds, recruiting young people for mission work, and giving talks on my mission experiences. But I now believed that the overwhelming economic and political interests of the United States in Latin America had contributed to the misery I saw. How could I speak of these realities to people in the States without alienating them?

At Thirty-six, Who Am I?

I joined a group of young people at the University of Minnesota who were active in promoting third world issues. Strangely, I had the impression that I had never left the university. I felt on my part that I still belonged there, that I was still like the students, and thought and felt like they did. I felt offended at the lack of reciprocity, that the students no longer regarded me as a fellow student. It was like a time warp. I was now thirty-six years old, a priest, an adult with a whole different perspective on myself and society. And students had changed, society had changed, people had changed from when I was last in St. Paul. We were no longer the same. My experiences in the seminary and Bolivia had radically formed me in vastly different values, customs, and perspectives. Who was I now, back in the United States, back where I had grown up?

Roy Bourgeois, now in Chicago, called and told me about an "arms bazaar" that was taking place in that city. He was organizing peoples from around the country to come and protest the wholesale promotion of weapons of violence and destruction in a very commercial "bazaar." We organized a busload of folks and drove to Chicago. The following day, we learned that Roy had been arrested for crossing the police line at the arms bazaar. This was my first experience with a friend getting arrested for protesting, and I didn't know what to do. Roy was released a day later. That was to be the first of many protests, arrests, and even jail time for this gentle prophet of justice for the poor.

The Third World Institute at the University of Minnesota had just launched a boycott of Nestlé's products to stop them from aggressively promoting bottle feeding of its powdered milk to poor mothers in third world countries. These women were given samples by Nestlé along with the company's sales pitch about powdered milk being better than breast feeding. When the poor women started their babies on powdered milk, their own milk dried up, but they could not afford to sustain their babies on infant formula. Nor could they adequately sterilize the bottles. The United Nations finally took up the cause with the theme "Breast Is Best" and the worldwide campaign forced Nestlé's to change its cynical advertising methods for selling infant formula in poor countries.

Together with other activists, we formed a Human Rights Working Group, which promoted the human rights proclaimed by the United Nations, especially of third world peoples. As part of the program, we hosted Isabel Allende, the niece of Salvador Allende, the president of Chile who died fighting against the coup of General Augusto Pinochet Ugarte. A woman called the Maryknoll house to protest us hosting a "communist" speaker. I told her that the Catholic bishops had already spoken quite strongly about the need to defend human rights. She snapped back that the bishops were all wet. Well, I said, even the pope was concerned about the plight of poor and oppressed people. She shouted, "The pope left the Church years ago!"

Goodwill Delegation from the USSR

A local human rights group told me of a goodwill delegation from the Soviet Union that would be visiting the Twin Cities in a few weeks, and they wanted to visit some ordinary families. This was still before the Berlin wall came down. The Soviet Union of Leonid Brezhnev was still alive and well. My mother and aunt both grew up speaking a mixture of Polish and Russian, and they agreed to invite a few of them over to the house for supper.

Arriving at the house, the guests, my mom, and aunt all burst into gab. After a hearty American meal and some vodka, Vasile Yagoli, a stout and proud bridge-building engineer with a bright red Lenin medal displayed on his lapel, explained to us that the two other guests were both members of the Moscow Symphony Orchestra and were some of the foremost musicians in Russia on the balalaika and accordion. So Anatolie Senia and Voldyrez Zlatimir hauled out their instruments and commenced to play a concert of Beethoven, right there in the cramped living room of the Newpower household. Mom has an organ, and they then asked her to play something. So she lit into the "Beer Barrel Polka." And it didn't take much for the guests to get up and dance. After some pictures, they departed and melted back into the cloud of Soviet anonymity. In 1989 the Berlin Wall came tumbling down, the Iron Curtain was shattered, and the communist threat melted into irrelevance.

■

Maryknoll, New York

AFTER TWO YEARS IN MINNEAPOLIS, Maryknoll invited me to the headquarters in New York to take over the Media Relations Department of the Society. The work would consist of producing educational materials on global concerns, a weekly syndicated radio program, a weekly TV program in the New York area, press relations for the Society, and producing films. I was tremendously interested, but felt I lacked experience. So they sent me to Hatch End, England, to a three-month-long radio and television workshop for Church people from Africa, Asia, and Latin America.

On March 24, 1980, I heard the news in London that Archbishop Óscar Romero of San Salvador had been gunned down at the altar while saying Mass. In his last Sunday sermon in the cathedral, he told the military to stop the killing. "Do not obey an order to kill your brothers and sisters. Rather obey the higher order of God to not kill." He was telling the soldiers to disobey their superiors, insubordination in the name of God! At his funeral, the military opened fire on the mourners as they processed out of the cathedral, killing thirty to fifty people. Romero had tried to be a voice for the voiceless. "If they kill me," he said, "my life will be seeds of liberty for the poor." The feature film *Romero,* released in 1989, described this man's conversion to the poor and showed his incredible courage. We at Maryknoll also produced a short film about El Salvador and Óscar Romero entitled *Seeds of Liberty*.

Archbishop Óscar Romero is depicted in this portion of a mural created in 2005 by Salvadoran artist Julio Reyes in the Monument to Memory and Truth.

In Bolivia, just two days before Romero's assassination, Jesuit Father Luís Epinal Camps was gunned down for criticizing the atrocities being committed by the military government of General García Mesa. Four months later, on July 17, 1980, the Mesa government also brutally assassinated Marcel Carriage Santa Cruz, an outspoken senator who was denouncing the corruption of the government and their links to narcotics. Marcel was a brilliant and humanitarian leader, who many believed would have been the best hope for a reasonable future for Bolivia. Many years later, ex-president Mesa was found in Brazil, brought back to Bolivia for trial and sentenced to life in prison for the torture and death of so many innocent Bolivian people.

Saddened by all the bad news, I visited the famous St. Paul's Episcopal cathedral in London to pray. The cathedral is incredibly huge. Viewed down the long central nave the altar seemed so far away. A ceremony was taking place there, but I couldn't see or hear what was going on. A man in a black cassock came down the central aisle with a pole and bag, asking for donations from visitors for the cathedral. It seemed my money could be better spent on those in need. And a few pews in front of me slouched a haggard old woman, who had come in from the cold to rest. I reached over and tucked some shillings into her hand. She awoke with a start and yelled at me. "What do you want with me? Leave me alone!" and began swearing at me. People were looking at us and I was embarrassed. That was the ironic thanks I got for my feeble attempt at charity.

Martyred in El Salvador, 2 December 1980
(l-r) Maryknoll Sisters Maura Clarke and Ita Ford, Ursuline Sister Dorothy Kazel, and lay missioner Jean Donovan.

Returning to Maryknoll from England, I had the opportunity to interview Maryknoll Sister Maura Clark for our TV program. She had just returned from her work in El Salvador, where Archbishop Romero had recently been gunned down. She told of the atrocities being committed by the military government against so many innocent poor people. Maura returned to her mission in El Salvador shortly afterward, and on December 8, 1981, her body, together with the bodies of three other Church workers, were found in a shallow grave near the road to the airport. They had been raped and murdered. The military government was blamed, as they were constantly threatening Church workers who associated and organized the poor, which Maura and her companions were doing. And all the while, the US government was providing $1.5 million a day to the Salvadoran government to fight "communism." Several years later, those actually responsible for the killings of the Sisters were brought to trial. But as expected, lowly soldiers were blamed, and the actual military authorities who ordered the atrocities had fled to Miami.

■

El Salvador Revisited

A FEW MONTHS AFTER THE SISTERS WERE KILLED, Maryknoll requested three of us priests to travel to El Salvador to report on the lives of the Maryknollers there.

We prayed at the tomb of Archbishop Romero in the cathedral and visited the simple room he occupied near a convent of Sisters. They showed us the blood-stained robes the archbishop was wearing when he was assassinated.

It was the first anniversary of the archbishop's murder. We traveled north to Ciudad Barrios, where he was born. Our Maryknoll host celebrated a special Mass for his anniversary, which was quite dangerous to do. After the Mass, an elderly woman who had known the archbishop personally, said to me that he was like Jesus, who did not die in due time of natural causes.

That evening, after going to bed, I heard a vehicle stop outside my window. I thought, this could very well be the military. They could just burst into the room and take me prisoner or kill me on the spot. Darkness and a strange place do such things to your mind. After a few minutes, which seemed like an eternity, the vehicle started up and moved on. I thought, this is the insecurity and fear that people live under every night in this country.

Our missionaries painted a depressing picture of the brutality of the government against anyone suspected of siding with the guerrilla movement, the Farabundo Martí National

Liberation Front (FMLN), which was seeking to topple the government.

One evening, returning to our church, we passed a body lying on the side of the road, decapitated. The priest told me there was nothing we could do about it, just forget it. An impression like that you cannot forget. It haunts you for years. I developed a sick taste for El Salvador. It seemed that an evil spirit had been unleashed in that society that demanded blood, not only blood but savagery to innocent people, God's precious, humble, innocent people. Ironically, the people who commit the evil and the people who suffer the consequences of that evil are not the same persons.

In one village, the people told me that the army came through and demanded the names of "subversives." They told their religious leader that they would be back in a few days, and if he did not give them three names of subversives in his village, they would kill him. So he said good-bye to his family and village. A few days later the army returned and killed this brave man who gave his life to protect his people. I wondered what possessed these military people to act so cruelly, and what would be the psychological affect or post-traumatic shock for them after this war finished.

The Suffering of the Innocent

St. Peter's reflections in his epistle reminded me that undeserved suffering, freely accepted in love, is always redemptive. Somehow, the suffering of the innocent, as Jesus, has a positive effect on others and the overall situation. This is the principle of nonviolence, taught and practiced by Gandhi and Martin Luther King Jr.

The brutal government repression in El Salvador lasted twelve years, until 1992, during which time more than seventy-five thousand were killed. The Arena Party continued to rule the country until 2009, when Mauricio Fuenes, a member of the Farabundo Marti National Liberation Front, the guerrilla group that had been fighting the government, was finally elected president.

A week after returning to the States from that trip, Roy

called me and asked me if the situation was real dangerous. A film crew from Chicago wanted Roy to accompany them to El Salvador as a translator. He went. Several days later, Maryknoll received a call from the US Embassy in El Salvador that Roy had disappeared. He had not kept a date with the film crew for a whole day and was not in his hotel room. We feared the worst. Newspapers in El Salvador reported that a Maryknoll missionary was missing. The army denied any knowledge of his whereabouts. The superior of Maryknoll traveled to El Salvador to investigate and even examine mutilated bodies. The press in the US hounded us for information about Roy, and as press officer, I had to respond. An agonizing week passed.

Then a call came from a reporter in El Salvador who read us a letter, apparently from Roy, that he had gone with the guerrillas to see the other side of the story. A couple of hours later, the US Embassy called us to say that Roy had shown up. Obviously he would be put on the next plane out of El Salvador. The Salvadoran military boarded his flight and ordered him off the plane. He refused, and some international reporters on the same flight filmed the conflict. The military finally relented and Roy headed for the States.

We checked schedules and realized that the plane would be arriving in Miami in several hours. We called an ex-Maryknoll friend in Miami who knew Roy, and asked him to meet the plane, get to Roy, avoid any reporters, and take him to his house until we could arrive.

We still did not know the details of what had happened with Roy nor his motives for disappearing. Maryknoll had a number of missionaries still in El Salvador and we did not want to jeopardize their work in that country. We dashed to the New York airport, got a flight to Miami and hours later entered the house where Roy was staying. He seemed a ghost, back from the dead. I held back tears to see my buddy alive and well, after fearing that he had been captured by the military, maybe tortured, and possibly killed, as so many others had been in El Salvador. He had lost weight and looked more gaunt and serious than I had known him to be.

Roy explained that the FMLN guerrilla group had invited him to join them for a week in the hills and experience firsthand the suffering of the rural peasants. He wrote a letter, which he left with the group, to be delivered the next day to the press after he was safely out of the capital. But the contact got scared by all the news about Roy's disappearance and he didn't release the letter for the whole week.

Now we wanted to avoid any advance publicity and get back to New York. The Maryknoll superior, who was traveling with us, told Roy that he could explain to the press his point of view in a press conference in New York, but the superior would also make clear that Roy acted as an individual and without permission from the Maryknoll Society. Roy's view would be taken into consideration, but he would not be suspended from Maryknoll nor the priesthood. Landing at La Guardia Airport in New York, we were met by a limo and taken to a special lounge for the press conference. The room was filled with some thirty reporters, who wanted to get the scoop on this renegade priest who took a walk with the guerrillas in the midst of a terrible war in El Salvador.

Roy later got wind that the US had transferred its military base in Panama to Columbus, Georgia. There, they were training military personnel from all over Latin America, presumably to defend their borders, but actually to fight subversion in their own countries. Roy began a protest movement at Ft. Benning, Georgia, that years later swelled to as many as twenty thousand participants. Protestors gathered each November 16, the anniversary of the slaughter in El Salvador of six Jesuit priests

Roy Bourgeois protesting outside the gates of Fort Benning, Columbus, GA, home of the US Army's School of the Americas.

Pilgrimage

and their housekeeper and her daughter. Most of the soldiers who participated in that massacre were graduates of the new School of the Americas in Columbus. Roy's lifetime commitment to justice for Latin America, was documented in 2004 in a book entitled *Disturbing the Peace*, by James Hodge and Linda Cooper.

Papal Visit

In 1983, Pope John Paul II visited the hot spots of Central America: Guatemala, El Salvador, Honduras, and Nicaragua. Maryknoll sent Fr. Steve DeMott and me to cover the visit and write some articles for our *Maryknoll* magazine and other news outlets.

Amid violence and martyrdom, a remarkable vitality characterized those churches. I visited a group of Salvadoran nuns who were preparing a banner of the slain Archbishop Óscar Romero to display in their meeting with the pope. They told me it may be dangerous to carry the image of Romero because the government detested him. But the visit of the pope gave them courage. I asked them why they would join a religious group during a time of Church persecution. They told me, "We grew up in poor barrios in San Salvador and participated in basic Christian communities. That experience inspired us to a vocation of service to the poor. We sneak back to our neighborhoods to visit the sick and console families whose members had disappeared. It's dangerous because paid informers report such activity to the police. This is now a Church of the catacombs, like in the early Church." In fact, more Christians have been mar-

Statue of Archbishop Óscar Romero in MacArthur Park Los Angeles, California.

El Salvador Revisited 127

tyred in Latin America over the last thirty-five years than all the Christians martyred by Rome in the first two centuries of Christianity.

Another Sister told me, "We share in the fear of the poor and the refugees. But this is an historic moment of grace and we are privileged to be witnesses of Christ's resurrection, even if it means giving our lives."

The pope visited the tomb of Archbishop Romero and praised him for having tried to halt the violence. Archbishop Romero was one of sixteen priests and religious women, including the two Maryknoll Sisters, assassinated in El Salvador over the six preceding years.

The papal visit to Guatemala was considered an intrusion by the military government of General Efraín Ríos Montt. He proclaimed himself a born-again Christian, but did not shy away from violently repressing the Mayan Indians, whom he considered subversives to his ruling party. On the road up to Quezaltenango to meet the pope, I noticed a sign: "Buy Indian handicrafts from us. We are widows of the war."

The pope addressed the violence: "Faith teaches us that human beings are the image and likeness of God. When their right to life is violated, a crime is committed against God." A million Mayan refugees had fled the death squad slaughters in the countryside of Guatemala, seeking refuge in the cities or wandering through the mountains and jungles to cross the border into Mexico. Seven years later I would meet up with them in a refugee camp in the Yucatan peninsula.

■

Films

OUR MEDIA OFFICE produced a number of films during this time, designed to share with people in the US our experiences and concerns, and hopefully build a greater solidarity in the world among all peoples. Roy collaborated with me in producing *Gods of Metal,* which showed the insanity of the nuclear arms race. The film was nominated for an academy award in 1982. Roy and I went to Hollywood to participate in the award ceremonies. This was the year that the films *Gandhi* and *Missing* both won several academy awards.

The production of other films took me to Zimbabwe, Korea, the Philippines, China, and Central and South America.

■

GODS OF METAL

And the Lord told Moses to say to the community, "Do not abandon me and worship idols. Do not make **gods of metal** and worship them. I am your Lord and God."
Leviticus 19

A NEW FILM BY MARYKNOLL ABOUT THE ARMS RACE

Achacachi Revisited

ON ONE OF MY OVERSEAS TRIPS I had the opportunity to return to Bolivia. I wondered if the folks would still remember me, or maybe even be angry with me. When I had departed, they told me I would never be back, like all the other priests who had come for a few years and then disappeared. No, I would be different. I would never forget them. So much suffering, pain, joy, and loving was lived in those seven years. I passed a lifetime there. I would be back, I thought. But now it was five years since leaving Achacachi, and I was now committed to work with Maryknoll in the States for a few more years.

Celebrating Mass in Achacachi, a wretched-looking elderly woman sat on the floor in the middle of the church by the first row of pews. She smiled and was obviously overjoyed to see me. I had forgotten about her. She had been in an automobile accident that had left her hobbling on a cane, unable to talk coherently, maybe a bit retarded or crazy or mentally incapacitated. Here she sat in her rags before me, and I in my clean, white alb, sitting on a throne, as it were. I was so touched by her crooked smile.

After Mass, I went down and embraced her. "You enthrall me, most wretched and poor woman. You are the embodiment of our God, helpless, defenseless, poor, alone, unattractive—yet smiling, with no hatred and no resentment." She could look up at me, someone who had far more than she could have ever dreamed of having: comfort, food, good looks, fine clothing, contentment, feelings of being esteemed, ten fingers, a clear voice, and straight legs. She forgave me, realizing, or maybe not realizing that having more does not mean being more. And that majestic gesture of greatness so touched me. It is that simple act that melts the most arrogant hearts, the power of the depraved victim, smiling love and forgiveness at those who are "other."

■

Companions

RETURNING TO NEW YORK, I met a Sister of Mercy who was studying at Maryknoll at the time. We became good friends. She had a deep and inquisitive spirituality, which we explored and pondered together over the next four years. This shared experience had a profound effect on my own spirituality.

I also met an elderly woman whom I had known years before while in the seminary. Annie Bennet had lived in a retirement community that I visited as a deacon to conduct worship ceremonies. Now she related to me her sad history. She was an orphan and grew up in a Salvation Army home in New York City. She had one brother, but had lost contact with him. She never knew what happened to him. Later she married, but did not have a happy marriage. They never had any children. After her husband died, she had no other family and ended up in a retirement home. She began going blind and in the process of being transferred to another facility, lost all her possessions.

In spite of this dismal history, Annie was a delightful woman. She said she was depressed after going blind, but decided in her faith to overcome her own personal grief, and try to live out the rest of her life more congenially with others. She would make up songs and sing them to me when I visited her. Often they were about us, as she fantacized that we were in love. She told me she had a dream one night in which we got married. But she said, "We didn't sleep together because I know that you are a priest and can't do that." Since she was blind, I bought her some flowers for her birthday, thinking that at least she could smell them and they would add a pleasant fragrance to her room. When I surprised her with the flowers, she said, "Get them out of her. I have hay fever!" As a remembrance, she gave me a beautiful picture of herself when she was younger. A few years later she passed to the great beyond.

Volunteering at a Local VA Hospital

Wanting to get out of the office, I began volunteering at a local hospital for Vietnam veterans. Poor guys and gals. Most of them had some mental problems, probably from post-traumatic stress, understandable, after participating in such atrocities. On my birthday, a man invited me to sit down and play chess with him. I don't know how to play chess, but thought maybe I could outwit this guy and win. He suggested moves for me, and finally said, "You win! It's your birthday, so I wanted you to win." The cordial virtues of those we sometimes judge to be beneath us or disabled in some way.

■

Archbishop Hélder Câmara

A REQUEST CAME TO MARYKNOLL ONE DAY to accompany Archbishop Hélder Câmara at our New York City house while he gave several conferences in the city. Archbishop Câmara was from a poor area in northern Brazil, and was a poor man himself, by choice. He embraced a simple lifestyle and the struggles of the poor. He was an outspoken critic of despotic governments that trampled on the lives of humble people, of which there were millions in his area. The dictatorial governments in Brazil and other parts of Latin America in the 1970s tried to silence any voices that clamored for justice, dignity, and respect for human rights. At the time Bishop Câmara had gained the reputation of being one of the "Red Bishops" of Latin America. He was also an influential voice for the poor at the Vatican Council in the 1960s and even more so at the Medellín Conference of Latin American bishops in 1968.

Archbishop Hélder Câmara, 1984

I was anxious to meet him, so I volunteered to accompany him for one of the days of his conference. He was a small man, coming only up to my shoulders. His face was wrinkled and big bags hung under his eyes. But his eyes, his eyes burned with a fire of unmistakable transcendence and love. He wore a beige cassock and a Roman collar. One cab driver in New York City kept looking in his rearview mirror at the bishop. Finally asked who he was. The bishop joked with him and it was apparent that the taxi driver was intrigued by his unusual visitor.

Statue of Archbishop Hélder Câmara in the Church of the Borders, where the archbishop lived for decades.

At the Maryknoll house, the archbishop wanted to say Mass. I prepared the altar, and waited for him to preside. But he said no, I should preside. He would assist me and be my altar boy. So this great champion of the Latin American poor, this famous author of several books on radical spiritual theology, stood humbly by my side, answering the prayers and pouring the wine for me to consecrate.

In the evening he asked me to help him prepare his talk. We worked for a short time and then he said he was weary and wanted to go to bed. He told me he usually woke up in the middle of the night, couldn't sleep and usually prayed for a couple of hours. I asked him for his blessing and knelt down before him. He then knelt down before me, and prayed over me. And then asked me for my blessing over him. This humble, gentle, spiritual man, so feared by unscrupulous dictators in Latin America, then retired to bed. At those moments, I felt so proud to be a spiritual brother to such an incredible man of God.

Embarrassing Moments

But often the role of a priest is inconvenient, uncomfortable, even embarrassing. One day, walking down 47th Street in New York City, I came across a woman lying on the street. I stopped to pick her up. Another man helped me lift her to her feet. At that moment, a bottle of liquor dropped out of her ruffled clothes. The other man helping her said, " Oh, she's drunk," and took off. So there I was, propping up this woman against the wall, hoping no one would recognize me. I asked her if she was all right, hoping she could take care of herself and I could get out of there quick. She said, "Pull up my pants!" That's all I needed to hear. "Come on, help me," she repeated. So I reached down and pulled up her pants. Then she said, "Buckle them!" Come on, lady. I don't need this. She seemed propped up and stable, so I took off, anxious to avoid any further embarrassment.

Another day on a bus from Washington, DC, to New York City, a young woman boarded after me, looked around for a seat, and came to sit beside me. She settled in and began jabbering about what a great time she had had over the weekend with her friends on a yacht, drinking, and soaking in the sun. She took out a book to read, one of those crotch novels. She told me she was thinking of writing one herself. Then she asked me what I did. I fumbled around for an answer. "Well, I work in South America." She was curious, and asked what I did there, and why I went there. "Are you a priest?" she finally asked. "Well, yes," I replied, somewhat uncomfortable with the whole situation. Her voice carried throughout the crowded bus, "Why didn't you tell me? Prove it! Show me some identification." Come on, lady. Everyone is looking at us and listening in on our conversation. Well, she finally shrugged, turned away in embarrassment, and began reading her book.

■

Spiritual Renewal

IN 1986, my term of office in the Media Relations Office was coming to an end. I was anxious to return to Bolivia. But first, I wanted to make a spiritual retreat. The Jesuits offered a month-long silent directed retreat north of Boston at their center in Gloucester, MA, overlooking the ocean. Every year during my priesthood I had made a retreat for a week and found those times incredibly enriching for my spirit, my body, and my mind. This time it took a few days to slow down into the silence and nothingness. But it became tremendously refreshing and spiritually nourishing to not only gain a deeper insight into my own journey, but also to become more attentive to the subtle whispers of the Spirit in my soul. The first day at the retreat two swans flew overhead, in perfect formation with one another. Could I be that sensitive to and move with the subtle movements of the Spirit at my side?

A Not Always Peaceful Journey
The spiritual journey is not always that peaceful. The Lord draws us out into the desert of our lives where we are tested. I began to realize that ambiguity and confusion are a natural part of being human. Jesus, hanging on the cross, cried out to his Father, "Why? Why me? Why this? Why now?" But he could only surrender his life in doubts. Eric Fromm, the great psychologist, once said, "Free man is by necessity insecure; thinking man by necessity uncertain."

> The great contemplative monk Thomas Merton's life was "filled with doubts and difficulties. Yet he clung to his faith, accepted his humanity, and shared in his writings a profound journey in darkness and light to God."

That was obviously the case with Fr. Thomas Merton, the great contemplative monk. His life was filled with doubts and difficulties. Yet he clung to his faith, accepted his humanity, and shared in his writings a profound journey in darkness and light to God.

In my journal, I described myself as an artist, prophet, and lover. Now I don't pride myself on being a great artist, but that is my bent, to try to express the inexpressible in artistic ways, whether in photographs, video, writing or any of the arts. Nor do I pride myself on being a great prophet, like those of the Old Testament. But that ministry attracts me, particularly the ministry of John the Baptist. He boldly denounced the evils in society and announced the Good News of the Reign of God present among us. That was my ideal. A lover? I hope I can always be a lover, lover of all of God's creation and all of God's creatures, especially those most in need. And finally to love myself.

■

Cuba

AFTER MY RETREAT, it was back to worldly activities. Maryknoll had received an invitation for someone to join a delegation traveling to Cuba. I jumped at the opportunity to experience firsthand the controversies about that little banana republic turned communist by the now famous Fidel Castro, with the aid of Che Guevara, the guerrilla fighter who was killed in Bolivia in 1968. The delegation met in Montreal, Canada, and a charter flight flew us to Havana. Obviously, the government showed us the brighter side of life in Cuba, but we were able to ask questions, mingle among regular people, and gain some sense of life in a socialist country.

At the end of the visit, President Fidel himself met with us. He entered the room and filled the space with his presence. He was a tall man, extremely at ease with us, confident, humorous, and obviously very well read. We asked him about religion and politics and his personal life. What an incredibly different viewpoint he had from all the right-wing dictators who were plaguing Latin America. He spoke of his commitment to the welfare of the common people on the island. Obviously there were scarcities because of the US blockade. But everyone had a job, everyone enjoyed free health care and free education. In comparison with the rest of Latin America, everyone in Cuba shared equally in the goods of society.

There was rationing so that everyone could have enough for their needs. Their wants and desires were a different story, and the reason some people would flee Cuba for the United

States. One sensed that life in Cuba was politically restricted. People could not criticize or demonstrate against the government. But that was the price the majority of poor people on the island were willing to pay to survive and gain an adequate living for their families. Most poor people in Latin America who live in misery envy their counterparts in Cuba. In comparison to the violence and massacres in Central America, Cuba was a holiday. Fidel entertained us for over an hour with his knowledge and wit and then thanked us for coming to experience firsthand the Cuban revolution.

One of our guides asked me if I would be interested in coming back for another visit and further conversations on the role of the Church in the US and in Latin America. I suppose it was because I was the only one in the delegation that spoke Spanish, and had struck up a nice friendship with our host. I told him I would talk with my religious superiors and let him know.

Back at Maryknoll headquarters, my superiors were open to the idea, especially since Maryknoll had received an informal invitation to work in Cuba. So I planned my return to Bolivia by way of Cuba, and also by way of Campeche, Mexico, where a dear friend, Maryknoll Brother Marty Shea, had invited me to join him for a couple of months in a refugee camp for Guatemalans who had fled the slaughter in their country.

Second Visit to Cuba

In my second visit to Cuba I was on my own. And I had a better opportunity to meet people and experience especially the life of the Catholic Church in Cuba. The archbishop of Havana, Jaime Ortega, was young, open, and politically astute. He received me warmly, as a representative of Maryknoll. We talked about the possibility of our coming to Cuba to work. He was very open to the idea, but of course, it would have to go through Vatican channels. Nothing later came of the invitation for Maryknoll to work in Cuba. Apparently the Vatican had reservations about the idea. The archbishop introduced me to some other clergy and then invited me to the Easter

Vigil celebration in the cathedral on Saturday evening.

Catedral de San Cristóbal, Plaza de la Catedral, Havana, Cuba (2009)

The cathedral in Havana enjoys a prominent location in the city, as do most cathedrals in Latin America, since the Church and Spanish governments were united in the conquest of this new continent. I arrived early, and many people had already gathered for Mass. The choir was practicing, a mixture of young and old people. I went to the sacristy to vest, and was warmly received by the other clergy who would concelebrate with the archbishop. They wondered who I was, and Maryknoll was known and esteemed by them. Then we processed into the church. The cathedral was filled, much to my amazement. The people of all ages eagerly joined in the singing to receive us, and I felt so proud to be a priest in Cuba in the midst of these people.

I met another gringo after Mass who said he was a reporter for the *Christian Science Monitor*. He looked very nervous, and told me as much, to be in Cuba for the first time, all alone and without much facility in Spanish. He felt people were watching him, and he was suspicious of the people he met for interviews. Poor guy. I was so thankful that I could speak Spanish and had found such a welcome among so many people.

One of the priests invited me to visit his parish and a few days later I was out on my own. I asked him if I could see a poor section of Havana. He paused and said there really weren't any. Actually, one section of his parish was rather modest in comparison. It was a neighborhood of the street sweepers and common laborers. He showed me around the area, and pointed out that everyone there had a job. Education and health care were free. We visited a clinic in which the doctor told me he knew the health situation of everyone in the neighborhood, particularly the smokers. Serious cases were referred to a bigger hospital in the city. Everyone had housing, though he conceded that the scarcity of adequate housing was still a problem in Cuba. I asked him about the difference in wages of a doctor and a street sweeper. He said a street sweeper would make about US$100 a month. A doctor would make about US$1,000, a ratio of ten to one. In a socialist country, wages are low, but most basic needs are taken care of by the government. So, he said, no misery, as is so blatant in Haiti and the rest of the Caribbean.

Cuba reminded me a lot of an Aymará village. There is obviously not a lot of room for dissent. There is strong pressure to conform, politically and socially. But the reward is belonging, having your basic needs met and the support of structures around you in case of emergencies. A non-conformist or non-sharing Aymará Indian is banned from the village. They live close to survival and cannot tolerate self-willed people who do not contribute to the common good of the community. This may appear to be rather harsh and restrictive, but the system works to provide for the needs of a majority of the members of that society.

Back at the hotel, I decided to go for an evening walk down to the ocean, close behind the hotel. When I returned, it was dark, especially behind the hotel. A young woman was walking toward me. I thought, either she is a hooker or else she may be afraid of me in this dark, isolated place. She walked right up to me and said, "Get off the grass!" What, did I hear you right? She repeated it, "Get off the grass. There is a sidewalk to walk on." And continued on her way. Wow! She wasn't a hooker, nor did she express the least bit of fear of encountering me in the darkness at that late hour. I wondered how characteristic her lack of fear was to ordinary life in Cuba.

■

Refugee Camp, Mexico

THEN I WAS ON TO MEXICO. Brother Marty Shea was waiting for me at the airport in the lovely Caribbean town of Campeche, on the Yucatan peninsula, home to many tourist resorts like Cozumel. We drove about two hours in from the coast, as the landscape became more and more arid and barren. There the Mexican government had given a section of land to be used for a refugee camp. About five hundred Guatemalan refugees now lived there, in rickety stick houses. The refugees had walked days and sometimes weeks through the mountains of Guatemala to cross the border and escape the massacres that were then taking place in their country. People in the camp were traumatized, sick, and weak. But they were clearly glad to be in a safe place.

Marty introduced me to a woman who had been catatonic for months. As a result of Marty's daily visits the woman felt safe enough to share her story with Marty about the murder she had witnessed of all of her family members.

We lived in a similar ramshackle house ourselves, next to a family who would cook for us. Campeche is unbearably hot. Temperatures in the afternoon were over one hundred degrees and everyone stayed indoors and rested. In the refugee camp, we were each allowed one pail of water, which was delivered in a tanker truck every day. I learned to shower with half a pail of water every afternoon.

Marty was wonderful with the people, just visiting them

Maryknoll Brother Martin Shea "was wonderful with the people, just visiting them and comforting them with kindness and a Word of God."

and comforting them with kindness and a Word of God. I became a little bored, and wanted to start up some programs, like a Bible study group or a daily prayer celebration. He said no. I was only there for a short time, and after I left, he could not continue my programs.

After two months, it came time to leave and I went around saying good-bye to my neighbors. One woman thanked me profusely for coming. I said, it wasn't much. After all, the Mexican Refugee Commission brought them food and water every day. "Yes," she replied, "but they don't care, like you do. We appreciate so much your concern for us and your kindness."

■

Bolivia Again

IT WAS TIME TO RETURN TO BOLIVIA, after almost ten years away. Maryknoll had closed out the parishes in Achacachi and the Altiplano and Joe Towle and Gene Toland had moved into La Paz and set up a video production studio.

I joined them, and we produced a series of four videos on Central America for high school students in the US.

In Nicaragua, we filmed Balty, a young Catholic woman who was studying medicine and working in a war zone. The new Sandinista government had just won a victory over the repressive Somoza government and had driven him out of the country. But the Contra fighters, with the help of the United States, were trying to topple the Sandinista government. Balty spoke about her commitment to faith and politics in a revolutionary society.

Fr. Joe Towle (center) with his sister and her husband pictured with Aymará parishioners in Achacachi, Bolivia.

In Guatemala we filmed Jeremías, an Indian boy, as he returned to his village, which the military had destroyed a few year earlier, massacring many of the inhabitants.

In El Salvador we filmed Flor, whose father and mother had been killed by soldiers. Flor fled to the city and participated in a youth group in her church.

In Honduras we filmed Carlos, a young man involved in a play for his neighborhood on the poverty and repression in his country.

Paul filming and editing in Cochabamba in 19??. Later, in La Paz, Paul worked with Fathers Joe Towle and Gene Toland to produce four videos on Central America for US high school students.

Hepatitis

Returning to Bolivia, I contracted hepatitis and had to spend six weeks flat on my back. Lying in bed I began to wonder if it had been a wise decision to return to Bolivia. My health was not good. I was tired and ornery. Again I consulted my superiors in New York, and they suggested I return to the States for a good checkup.

■

USA Again

MARYKNOLL WAS EXTREMELY GENEROUS in giving me a long break for some needed physical and personal recovery time. I guess life had been a little too hectic and intense and I needed some time to step back and see where I was at. I began to realize that I had bitten off more than I could chew.

I began wondering if all the hours spent in prayer and contemplation over the years had been worthwhile, whether they had made any difference in my life and self-awareness. Well, maybe they did, because without them, without that long retreat, maybe I would never have gotten to this point in my life. It just took a while to sink in.

The dark side, my shadow side, with all my failings, had always been an enigma to me. I knew I wasn't perfect, that I had my faults, my sins. Sometimes I even felt an inclination to flirt with that which I knew was wrong, a disturbing tendency to evil, which really scared me. Where does that come from? I wondered if maybe we humans were basically bad, but with some good tendencies. Or if maybe we were basically good, but with some bad tendencies. As a person of faith, I believed the latter, that God created us basically good. But with the freedom to choose the bad. A mystery. The dilemma of St. Paul encouraged me. He wrote of a personal weakness: "I begged the Lord three times to take it away, but He responded: My strength is sufficient for you, for my strength is made manifest in your weakness."

With some help, I also began to realize that I was living outside of myself, living on the expectations of others, trying too hard to perform for them. I was overly concerned about my image and was losing touch with my own emotions and needs. Thanks be to God and the support of so many wonderful people around me that drew me along and gently lifted me back into a more healthy state of mind, body, soul, and spirit. But I still wondered about my future.

Hunger Strike

Meanwhile, Roy Bourgeois was staging a hunger strike in the cathedral in St. Paul, MN, to press the US bishops to speak out against the repressive role of the US in Central America. He had rallied a great following and was calling for others to undertake similar protests. I wondered about jumping back into an activist life or holding off for a while more to take care of my own needs. But at the end, I felt it was time. I was feeling much better about myself and was still terribly concerned about the situations in Central America. So I traveled to Washington, DC, and joined a hunger strike at the Episcopal church President George Bush attended. We fasted on water alone for seventeen days. We hoped we were contributing in some way to the campaign to oppose government support for cruel dictators in Central America.

After the strike, I moved in with a group of Jesuit priests, living in a poor, Black neighborhood in DC. I wanted to stay

Paul (holding umbrella) at a protest demonstration in Washington, DC.

and help organize a commemoration event in Washington for the anniversary of the martyrdom of Archbishop Romero.

The first night with the Jesuits, we heard some gunfire. I ventured out to find that it was a drive-by murder a block away from our house. Great welcome! The next day, I asked the priests where I could catch a bus to go downtown. They gave me directions and bracing myself I headed out on the streets. Turning the corner to the bus stop, I saw a group of Black men sitting on a stoop. They spotted me. Oh, oh, I thought. So I put on my serious face and tried to strut boldly past them. One of them called after me, "Hey buddy, hey buddy!" Should I ignore him? Run? Well, I turned, and he said, "How come you're so glum? It's a nice day. Cheer up!" Once again, I was surprised by the cordiality of people I tended to fear.

Back to Bolivia?

Returning to the Maryknoll Center in Ossining, NY, I continued to ponder my future. Some people were counseling me to stay in the States and even explore some other options in life. But something made me want to return to Bolivia. I believe it was the radically different lifestyle and values there that attracted me, a slower pace of life, less aggressiveness, less materialism, less consumerism, and a more homey and friendly atmosphere. I always felt safe walking the streets in Bolivia, even during the times of political upheaval. Even God seemed more real there. The only problem was the anguish I always felt in my soul for the undeserved suffering of so many innocent people. But it was a hurt that seemed Jesus himself experienced during his brief sojourn on this earth. Mission was now in my soul, and I wanted to join in solidarity with people who were poor and struggling for a more dignified life. Maryknoll agreed for me to return, so it was back to Bolivia again.

■

Cochabamba

CHE GUEVARA ONCE SAID: "I have renounced what are the most sacred things to a person—their family, their country, their surroundings." Why would a person give them all up? For a certain sense of adventure. But more.... For me, the most profound sense was spiritual. It was an attempt to separate myself from those aspects that seemed most dear and move in a direction of less clinging to what society has to offer for happiness. It is a strange movement—to renounce what seems most dear in an attempt to find something even more profound, more dear, more meaningful, more worthwhile. And yet that something more dear always remains just a little out of reach.

A Restless Heart

As St. Augustine said: "My heart is restless until it rests with you, my God." I feel that restlessness, a certain lack of fulfillment. But at the same time, I know that I'm closer to the truth, on the right path. There are glimmers of fulfillment that truly stir my soul, give me profound joy and a sense of peace that I do not find in all the enticements around me. And what is it? A feeling of sharing with others, that I matter, am significant to somebody...and ultimately to God. And not for what I *do*, but simply because I *am*.

In Bolivia, Gene Toland and Joe Towle had moved on and no other Maryknollers were stationed in La Paz. So I opted to return to Cochabamba to set up a video production studio there and engage in some pastoral work.

Many of the other Maryknoll priests in the Cochabamba area and in the rest of Bolivia were older now and had borne the heat of long missionary careers. I found them were less enthusiastic about Maryknoll's great missionary adventure in Bolivia. I, however, was at a different point in my life. I still hoped I could enthusiastically embrace a new beginning to my missionary vocation.

In Cochabamba, Fr. Tom McBride, a kind and gentle elderly Maryknoll priest, invited me to join him in the large inner-city parish of Cristo Rey. One afternoon behind the church, I happened upon a group of students who were practicing a skit together. When I asked what they were doing, they said, "Don't you know? Tomorrow is May 1, International Labor Day. We are practicing a play about the Chicago massacre, when so many workers were killed protesting for an eight-hour workday and the right to organize in unions." Oooops! I guess that incident had not been a part of my education.

Rolando's Story

Shortly after getting settled in, a priest friend from Chile contacted me and asked if I might visit someone in jail in Cochabamba. A family member had told him that their brother had gone to Bolivia looking for work and ended up in jail. He had no family or friends around to help him. I presented myself at the jail and asked to see Rolando. The guard opened a big ancient wooden door and I entered into a mass of men mingling around a central courtyard, surrounded by three stories of dilapidated housing. It was truly abominable! The jail was an old converted colonial mansion where 437 men were crowded into a place meant for a comfortable family. There were only two bathrooms. New arrivals had to sleep on the floor until a room or cot became available. I asked some of the inmates for Rolando and they joked, "Oh, you mean the Chilean guy." Chilean people are often denigrated in Bolivia because of a war Chile waged during the last century in which they stripped Bolivia of its seacoast.

I located Rolando and he told me his version of his story. I learned later that he was quite a notorious criminal. He had been jailed on drug charges, released, got high again, and boarded a bus while the driver was absent. He drove the bus through an intersection, crashed a taxi, and killed the driver. So now he had a homicide charge hanging over his head.

But poor guy, the locals frequently beat up on him for killing an innocent Bolivian and for being a brazen Chilean. He was one of those sleeping on the floor outside. So, according to jail custom, I bought a room for him. It wasn't much, barely room for a cot. He later rented out space on the floor next to the cot to another inmate for a little spending money. The jail provides some meager food, but most inmates buy more substantial food from the vendors around the courtyard.

I tried to intervene for Rolando but the legal system in Bolivia is woefully slow and unjust. Most of the men had never even been sentenced. I pleaded for him, but to no avail.

I tried to visit Rolando every week and bring him some food or medicine, but the visits were always incredibly depressing. I had a terribly hard time going back each time, and frequently allowed myself to be distracted by some other activity. Poor Rolando. He was just languishing in that jail.

After Christmas I went to the jail, but he was no longer there. They told me he had been depressed, started drinking on Christmas Eve, which is tolerated in that loose detention facility, and drank himself to death. His family contacted me, inquired about coming to claim the body, but in the end they never came. I always felt guilty that I didn't visit Rolando on Christmas and bring him some food for the holiday.

Pastoral Work…Again

Fr. Tom and I discussed the pastoral work that I could do in the Cristo Rey parish. I told him that I wanted to live closer to the people, not isolated in a rectory, to share more closely in their lives, walk with them more as a brother than as a traditional priest. He suggested a far corner of the parish that was largely unattended, Villa Bush. He told me that two young

Pastoral team, 1975. (r-l): Fr. Paul Newpower, Fr. Gene Toland, Fr. John Gorski, Fr. Paul O'Brien, Fr. Joe Towle, and Br. David McKenna. Seated are staff members Maria Irma Viscarra Valda, Frida Juana Conde Aduviri, Paula Aduviri Mamani de Chuquimia, and Enrique Aduviri Mamani.

lay missionary women had recently moved into the area. The support of a priest would be very helpful to them. With that suggestion, Fr. Tom had unwittingly opened a door to my future destiny. Brother David McKenna (pictured above) was also looking for a place to live, so he and I moved into a small house in the area.

■

Rebeca

REBECA WAS ONE OF THE YOUNG WOMEN beginning pastoral work in Villa Bush, so we began visiting homes and organizing religious activities together. People thought we were Evangelicals, but were happy to find out that we were Catholics and were there to minister to their faith. We formed Basic Christian Communities, small groups of people who would come together in someone's home once a week to pray, study Scripture, and share their daily struggles. Eventually, they built themselves a Church. They wanted me to build it, but I said I was there only to plant the seed, to get them started. I was not a builder of monuments. So they did it themselves, and finally, after having celebrated the Eucharist in empty lots and homes for five years, we had our own chapel, with the name "Christ of Forgiveness." We had formed adult leaders who now were committed to their faith and wanting to spread it. We had formed many children to receive the sacraments. We had formed young people to consider other values in life than the superficial values offered by society.

During that time, Rebeca and I became companions in the ministry. People knew that and respected us.

Rebeca had had a rough upbringing in Potosí. Her dear and loving mother died when she was eleven and her strict father when she was eighteen. Her three brothers ended up treating her as their maid. She had been active in her church and a priest there gave her a Bible and encouraged to move on and find a life of her own. She ended up a few years later in Cochabamba as part of a Bolivian missionary association. She lived with a Maryknoll Sister in a rural area and walked the hills to visit isolated Indian villages with the Word of God. The Maryknoll Sisters wanted her to join their Order, and encouraged her to continue her academic studies. She decided on a career in social work and enrolled in a five-year program at the university. In 1999 she graduated as the first social worker from that university.

One day I received a call from Rebeca's older brother in Potosí saying that her younger brother, Abel, whom she loved dearly, had just died of meningitis. Rebeca was coming over to my house a short while later and I waited for her in anguish. She burst in the door with her usual sense of joy, but quickly read the grief on my face. One of the hardest things I have ever had to do was to tell her this tragic news.

To Potosí...with Rebeca

Rebeca asked if I might accompany her to Potosí to assist at the funeral. In Bolivia, people are still waked in their homes all night in the presence of family and neighbors. The next day we walked the hour behind the funeral car to the cemetery and laid poor Abel to rest. Rebeca and I went to his room and sorted through his belongings. He had been a rural school teacher, but lived alone and apparently did not take good care of himself. As is the custom in Potosí, we also had to dispose of all his belongings, taking them to the outskirts of the city and burning them.

Video Productions

WHILE PERFORMING PASTORAL WORK, I also continued to work in communications, producing video programs with the equipment that we had used in La Paz. The Franciscans in Cochabamba contracted with me to produce several TV spots on social themes. We produced one on the litter in the city caused by the excessive use of plastic bags. We had an actress walk through the market carrying two plastic bags filled with groceries. She stepped on a plastic bag (coated with honey) which stuck to her shoe, and which she couldn't scrape off with her other shoe. A plastic bag then flew into her face, guided by thin fishing lines with wind from a fan with a long extension cord through the open air market. She became angry, shrugged, and the two bags of groceries broke open, emptying their contents on the ground. The next scene showed her returning to the market to buy groceries with a cloth bag, not plastic.

TV Videos for the Archdiocese

We created TV spots for the archdiocese, especially to highlight Holy Week. To illustrate the Resurrection, we arranged for a man to come walking down the street and knock on a door. Inside, a girl woke up and said to her mom, "Mommy, I think daddy has come back home." They go outside, and have a tearful reunion, like Jesus back from the dead.

We also produced several religious videos, illustrating the local Urqupiña festival, which attracts over three hundred

The Urqupiña festival attracts over three hundred thousand every year to commemorate what is believed to be an apparition of the Virgin Mary to some peasant children a couple of hundred years ago.

thousand every year to commemorate what is believed to be an apparition of the Virgin Mary to some peasant children a couple of hundred years ago.

And we filmed the Santa Vera Cruz festival, where thousands of indigenous people gather every year in a fertility rite so their animals might have many healthy offspring. The Catholic Church, as it has done throughout history for many secular celebrations that it considered pagan, tried to replace it with a religious celebration. So today, the fertility rite is still culturally celebrated, but on the feast of the Holy Cross on the grounds of the church. The two traditions continue now with a symbiotic relationship.

Since we were working in film productions, a friend of mine in New York, Bob Richter, asked me to organize a segment of a film for him on the role of the World Bank and the International Monetary Fund in Bolivia. Those institutions had pressured the Bolivian government to sell off all state-owned industries, as a way of generating currency for a poor economy. In 1984 the Paz Estenssoro government had sold off extensive state-owned tin mines. As a result, thousands of poor miners were laid off and migrated to the misery of the cities or to the Chapare valley to grow coca leaves, as a way to survive and be able to eat. But coca leaves are the primary ingredient for producing cocaine. So the net result of the IMF and WB policies was to increase the drug production of cocaine in Bolivia. The title of the film we helped make was titled *Hungry for Profit*.

Indigenous Traditional Wisdom

An old friend of mine from Achacachi, Genaro Clares, also asked us to film the first congress in Bolivia of "Indigenous Traditional Wisdom." But he cautioned me that the group might not want a gringo outsider invading their sacred deliberations. So my Bolivian video assistant went first to break the ice, and I came later to help him out.

What an incredible experience to participate with those Aymará and Quechua elders as they discussed ways to revive their traditional teachings. So unlike government propaganda or the pious platitudes of so many Church people, they spoke of integrating the male and female gender elements, of integrating political and religious beliefs, of integrating the social and economic orders of their societies. They spoke of harmonizing the many different areas of life for the mutual benefit of everyone. One of the elders ended the conference by encouraging the participants to revive their traditional values for the good of all humanity, saying "We are infinite."

■

Wedding Bells

FINALLY MY SIX-YEAR PASTORAL ASSIGNMENT in the neighborhood and my video production work was coming to an end. Again I was faced with what to do next. The Maryknoll General Council published a document in 1995 called "Journeying in Hope and Trust." In the document they stated: "The context of mission today offers radically different challenges that call for creativity, integrity and authenticity. Tried and true methods may no longer suffice.... New paradigms are still to be born.... Each of us appropriates the Maryknoll spirit in new and creative ways, not without tensions and misunderstandings, but with the firm conviction that this is the direction the Spirit is calling us to take. One can no longer be content to remain with what existed before. Everyone is called to venture beyond their safe space.... The first journey in mission is merely a preparation for the second. Embracing these values invites not only persecution and risk, ambiguity, and uncertainty, but also an infinite amount of new opportunities and creativity to search for and discover Christ among all of God's peoples." Those words gave me the courage and trust I needed to consider a dramatic change in my life in mission.

I certainly wasn't getting any younger, and if I had any inkling of moving on from the priesthood and starting a new life, then I'd better not wait too long. Rebeca and I had become close over the years, and we shared many values in our faith, in our commitment to the poor, in the cultural realities of Bolivia, in seeking a simple lifestyle in prayer and solidarity with those in need. We had struggled through a lot of ambiguity in our relationship, but in the end, realized we really cared for one another. I seriously considered for the first time in my life the real possibility of leaving the priesthood and getting married. I prayed about it and talked it over with my family and with some friends I thought would understand. The more we talked, the more that direction seemed right for me at that time in my life. And the more it seemed that God was calling me in this direction for a new mission paradigm.

A Proposal, I Guess...

Finally one day I spoke to Rebeca about my thoughts. I guess I asked her if we might consider getting together, you know, like joining together as a couple, maybe getting married.... I guess I proposed! It would mean that we would not separate now, that we would continue and deepen our relationship into the future, that our ministries would now move in new directions. We talked and talked about the possibility. We realized we loved one another and it seemed right for us to take this dramatic step into the unknown. It seemed that God was with us and leading us down an uncharted pathway. Our hearts felt good about it, and we both said yes. We worried about getting a job, about supporting ourselves, about where we would live, about what our friends would say, about staying in Bolivia. But in spite of it all, we wanted to take the step and make the commitment to one another, trusting that God would see us through the difficulties. With that confirmation full of ambiguity, I finally spoke to a Maryknoll superior. He was understanding, but requested me to return to the States for consultation.

Ironically, at the time, my brothers called to tell me that my father was dying. Could I come home right away. I immediately booked a flight and on the plane wondered if I would arrive in time to see him again. Maybe I could assure him that the angels were waiting for him, to not be afraid. I fell asleep on the plane and dreamed that I was at a party with a lot of family and friends. There was a tall, elderly man there that I did not know. I asked him who he was. He said, "I came to accompany your dad to the great beyond." The angels weren't waiting for him. They were already at his side to accompany him on the journey. I arrived in time, was able to say good-bye, and whispered to him that I was planning on getting married. Mom was at his side as he slipped away, and Rebeca in Bolivia had a premonition at the time of his passing. I was still in good standing with the Church and was able to celebrate the Mass and bless his final resting place.

Paul and Rebeca in their home in Maplewood, MN.

After the funeral I needed to go to Maryknoll, NY. I went feeling a great deal of anxiety about seeing my brother Maryknollers. They would surely not look kindly on my getting married. It was like leaving a family; worse, like breaking a long-standing loyalty, a bond that most everyone expected would last a lifetime. It would mean suspension from my active ministry in the priesthood. It would mean separation from Maryknoll, both economically and personally.

But nothing is forever, and we, Rebeca and I, felt deeply that God was calling us to a different lifestyle, a different ministry. And it was a call we did not want to miss, no matter the risks involved. In my diary I wrote: "I pray, Loving Spirit, your sacred help and sustenance for this mysterious venture that I am so reluctant to embrace, yet so anxious to realize."

Leave of Absence

At Maryknoll, I requested a leave of absence from my ministry. This is granted initially without formal separation from Maryknoll as a time of discernment. Maryknoll wanted me to leave Bolivia for a year to decide what I wanted to do with my life. But in no way was I interested in leaving Rebeca nor Bolivia. We had already decided! I didn't need any more time for discernment. But I agreed to step back from my ministry and Maryknoll and explore life outside the fold of religious life, in Bolivia.

I had grown accustomed to the country and the people and the culture. I enjoyed living in a small, poor, insignificant country, like Jesus. Besides, it is a beautiful country, with towering snow-capped mountains in the Andes and deep, dark jungles in the Amazon. It is also home to ancient Indian civilizations, like the Incas. The people are traditional, homey, and friendly. Strangers still greet you on the streets. People seem to have time for one another. The pace of life is slower here.

Yet the people are actively involved in seeking dramatic changes in society, revolutionary changes, and that excites me. They know that what has transpired for the past five hundred years has not worked for the majority, and they are struggling to come up with a better alternative. It is not easy and is often conflictive with the old ruling elite, who have carved out a very comfortable lifestyle for themselves here. But one thing worried me about staying in Bolivia and that was getting a job, because the country's poverty limits many job opportunities, especially for foreigners.

Before getting married, Rebeca and I went around together and told people whom we thought were our friends that we were planning to marry. To our surprise, some of those whom we thought were our closest friends and who would have been most supportive of our marriage were actually quite shocked and dismayed. Some even consulted with a priest and were advised not to associate with us.

Others whom we thought would react negatively were actually very supportive and wished us well. Rebeca was worried that people would blame her for stealing a priest away from his vows, at least that was a common notion in Bolivia. But Bolivia has few celibate priests. The majority seem to have a woman and children, putting up a front that the woman is a relative or housekeeper, without making any formal declaration of marriage. People know. The bishops know. And they all look the other way. It is hypocrisy, but it functions for maintaining the functional role of priesthood in society.

We were married in a civil ceremony on January 27, 1996. Initially we wanted to have a quiet, somewhat private ceremony. But so many people wanted to come that we eventually rented a hall and catered a meal.

Was I nervous? Well, yes, I guess I was. Not frightened nor worried about our future together. I figured our relationship was solid, and I was really excited about beginning this new phase of my life. I guess it was something I had always had in the back of my mind, to live a normal life, be a normal person, with no pretensions. To join the human race in all its struggles and joys. The missionary documents of Maryknoll always encouraged us to seek ways to become more acculturated into the cultures where we lived, to seek to identify more closely with the common people in our ministries. Well, this seemed like a very good way of becoming acculturated into the Bolivian mainstream, to become as much as possible a part of it. Wasn't this mission, something cross-cultural, going to a different country, a different society, a different culture, and witnessing to the universality of God's love, that we are all sisters and brothers who share in the same destiny? We are one. That was Jesus' final prayer, "That all may be one, Father, as you and I are one, they in me and You in me, as I am in You." I have never regretted taking that step.

A few hundred people came for the wedding. The hall was packed. And in walked Rebeca, dazzling in

Wedding day, January 27, 1996

Wedding Bells 163

Rebeca and Paul with friends on their wedding day.

her long white dress and looking so pretty. She walked up to the front amidst the applause of all the guests. The cameras rolled. The notary public talked too long. We exchanged our vows and recited a prayer of commitment sent to me by Fr. William Wilson of the Amistad Mission, who had married a few years earlier.

From Achacachi came Fr. Julio Rojas, the first Aymará priest ever ordained and a very dear friend. He said a blessing over us, which was much like the official Catholic ceremony. Some thought that he had married us.

Then we danced and danced and ate and drank and danced. The ceremony had been scheduled for six o'clock, and I had wondered what everyone would do for the rest of the evening. Not to worry. The time flew by. At two o'clock in the morning they wanted to close the hall. So we set off outside on foot, about twenty of us, led by Jim Parker, the only one to come from the States. We danced and sang, Rebeca in her wedding gown and I in my suit, down the streets of Cochabamba. Young people still enjoying the warm night clapped as we danced by. We piled into some taxis with all of our family and friends and went home. About ten people slept over, crowding onto whatever floor space they could find in our house.

■

Getting a Job

AFTER OUR MARRIAGE, I expected that I would continue working with my video project. Maryknoll had given all of the video equipment that I had used for the past six years to the archdiocese. Initially Church authorities in Cochabamba seemed amenable to having me collaborate with them in utilizing the equipment for their pastoral activities. But came the day of our wedding and they locked the door on me, literally. Orders from Archbishop René Fernandez! They would not even let me enter that room and recover any of the video tapes of programs I had produced over the past six years. Never had I come so close to violence than at that moment, feeling so helpless and so unjustly excluded.

I talked with the archbishop and he assured me that things could be worked out. But nothing came of his promises. I talked with the Maryknoll superior, but he did not want to confront the archbishop. I hired a lawyer, but she had the archdiocese as a client and did not want to step on anyone's toes. For three long months I waited before they finally let me into the office accompanied by the Maryknoll superior, who did not want to be there, and I quickly recovered what was still there of my personal belonging.

So I was out of work, really. Rebeca was still studying at the university, so we needed some income. I began pestering any contacts I knew, and finally an ex-Maryknoller, Dudley Conneely, offered me a job in his organization, Project Concern International. Dudley who was a couple of years behind me in the seminary, came to Bolivia and worked in the Santa Cruz area. A couple of years later he married a Bolivian woman and stayed on, working in different projects in Bolivia. This was truly a godsend for me. However, the job was in Santa Cruz. I ended up commuting back and forth on weekends to Cochabamba to be with Rebeca, taking a twelve-hour overnight bus ride.

Project Concern

Project Concern worked on rural development, building roads into isolated villages, constructing potable water projects to bring an aspect of hygiene to the primitive lives of rural peasants, and providing food aid as an incentive for them to contribute manual labor to the projects.

Interestingly, I brought my Maryknoll work ethic into the job, and it did not fit. In Maryknoll, we would try to promote other people to be leaders and would personally stay in the background. In my new job, word was that Newpower wasn't doing anything and that those who worked with him were pulling all the load. I began to learn that I needed to toot my own horn, be more aggressive and up front with my superiors about what I was doing. Fortunately, the project opened a branch in Cochabamba, and I was able to move back home to be with Rebeca.

Amistad Association

After a couple of years with Project Concern, I received a call from the States from Fr. William Wilson, a Trappist monk who had worked in Bolivia during the 1980s and founded an orphanage, the Amistad Association. He then returned to the States, married, and joined the Episcopal Church. He now needed someone in his Bolivian project to do religious education with the children, to take care of visitors from the States and to act as a liaison between the project in Bolivia and the board of directors in the States. In my work with Project Concern, I missed the religious dimension, and this seemed right up my alley. So I joined the Amistad Association in Bolivia. After Rebeca finished her degree in social work, and after a few years working with other projects, she joined me in Amistad, first as religious coordinator and then as the social worker.

■

Family

IN 2000 TRAGEDY AGAIN STRUCK OUR FAMILY as I received word that Rebeca's older brother, Elias, had been killed in an automobile accident in Oruro. Again, I had to break the awful news to Rebeca and it was a horrible shock to her. She had grown very close to Elias and he often visited us in Cochabamba. We also traveled to Potosí several times to visit with him, his wife, and three children. Everything stopped. We took the next available bus to Oruro, a five-hour ride, and arrived in the evening for the all-night wake. Rebeca and Elias's family were so distraught. The next day, we arranged for the body to be brought to Cochabamba where he would be buried. Again, we waked him in our house for the night and buried him the following day.

Rebeca and I talked about having children. One day, she came home from work with a frail three-year-old girl, whose mother was dying of cancer. She wondered if we might take her in for a few days. Then she was off to classes at the university. Anabel began to cry...and cry and cry. I sang all the nursery songs I could remember, but she was not comfortable in the arms of a strange man. Finally, a girlfriend of Rebeca's came by to visit, took Anabel and calmed her down until Rebeca returned. Anabel stayed with us for a few years until one of her sisters agreed to take responsibility for her. We still see her a lot, especially for her birthdays, when she comes to our home.

In 2001 our first child was born and we named him Elias,

An early photo of the Newpower family:
Paul, Elias, Rebeca, and Rosie.

in memory of Rebeca's dear brother. Three years later Rosie came along, whom we named after my spunky ninety-one-year-old mother in St. Paul. Here I was, a father of two little children at sixty-three years of age. Life just unfolds that way, and you go with the flow. I have no regrets. I thoroughly enjoyed my twenty-five years as a Maryknoll missionary priest. And I am thoroughly enjoying my years now as a regular family man. It is just what was missing in my life. Not a minute available now to be lonely. The house is full of laughter and children quarreling and all the little daily routine activities that keep one so busy.

So many of my previous anxieties have diminished, only to be replaced by others of a more domestic kind. But now I have a partner to share them with, and two lovely children who yank me back to this reality with their needs for affection and reassurance. I never used to worry about anything, even death. But now life seems so much more precious to me and for my family. I worry now for what sometimes seems a precarious future. But God is good. I only pray for confidence that God will see us through anything that may come our way.

■

Bolivian Politics

ONE FINAL POINT is the politics in Bolivia at this point in my writing.

To the astonishment of everyone, an Aymará Indian by the name of Evo Morales was elected president of the country in 2005. This was the first time in the history of Bolivia that an indigenous person was elected to the presidency, in a country where 70 percent of the population is Indian. He won with 54 percent of the popular vote, again a margin never achieved in Bolivian history. What happened?

The people were fed up with the corruption of the traditional ruling parties, a small elite who had exploited their power for personal gain. A recent president, Gonzalo Sánchez de Lozada was driven out of the country in 2003. He ended up in New York City with $200 million in his pocket. The voters also saw in Evo Morales a refreshing new vision, calling for a reorientation of the country to favor the majority of the population, who were poor, workers, and Indians. He responded to a call by those peo-

Evo Morales, the first Aymara Indian ever elected president of Bolivia.

President Evo Morales and his Cabinet.

ple to rewrite the Constitution of the country, away from structures and an ideology based on personal gain, and in favor of redistributing the scarce resources of the country for the common good.

Once elected, he began renegotiating the contracts with the oil and gas companies, which tripled the income to the country. This additional income was redistributed to school children and the elderly. The basis of the new economic policies is that all citizens who had been excluded from the economy would now "live well," rejecting a free market economy in which a few people had all the advantage and accumulated huge personal wealth.

Obviously, these changes did not set well with the elites of the old ruling parties. They have been fighting Evo Morales tooth and nail. They cannot accept that an "Indian" now sits in the presidential chair, one of those uneducated, uncivilized peons who until recently only served as their dutiful servants. Who knows how this will all turn out. But for now it is the dawning of a new age for the millions of people in Bolivia who have been exploited and discriminated against for five hundred years. The people feel it. They know this is a unique and historic opportunity, not only for Bolivia, but for all the nations of Latin America, which have suffered a similar fate.

The Pilgrimage Continues

AND HERE I AM, an immigrant as my ancestors had been, still journeying in a strange land. I yearn to belong here, to fit into the culture and be accepted and appreciated, to feel that I matter to others around me, that I am worthwhile and can contribute something to my surroundings. I long to blend into the culture and the people, and not have people ask me where I am from. But my accent betrays me and people often initially speak loud to me, thinking that will help me understand what they are saying. My looks also betray me and I stand out like a sore thumb among all the dark Latin and Indian people of Bolivia. For as hard as I try, I am still an outsider in Bolivia and my roots are still in the States. I spent my first twenty-eight years growing up in the US culture and speaking English. One does not leave that heritage behind. I have a foot in both cultures and can never escape the ambiguity of not really belonging here nor probably belonging any more back in the States. But when people learn that I have been here for twenty-five years and have a Bolivian wife and family, they generally accept me and reassure me that I am now a part of the culture.

A New Missionary Witness

What about my missionary witness? Well, it seems it now blends in with a rather normal life. My faith witness is now as a family. We struggle along with other people to make ends meet. We suffer many of the same hardships of health and

The Newpower family in 2022. Paul and Rosie seated. Rebeca and Elias standing.

insecurity and inadequate income. We share with others in a trust that God will provide. I enjoyed my ministry with the Amistad Mission and the orphanage. Rebeca still shares that ministry as their social worker. We developed a Good Samaritan Ministry to provide emergency funds to people in crisis situations.

The plight of the poor and living close to them in their sufferings causes an anguish in my heart that does not go away. But hopefully our faith in a loving God shines through and even brightens up the lives and struggles of others. And hopefully our lives and our resources shared with others in this little corner of the world, might in some small way contribute to the unfolding of the reign of God among us, a reign of peace, of understanding, of compassion for the poor, of love and respect for one another. Our heartfelt hope is that more and more everyone will learn to live together on this small planet earth as sisters and brothers.

Appendix 1

The Long Road from Cochabamba to Minnesota

An *Interchange* interview with Paul Newpower ('69)

Interchange (IC): You were assigned directly to Bolivia after your ordination in 1969, correct? And you spent most of your years of missionary service there.

Paul Newpower (PN): Yes, my first assignment was to Bolivia. I had requested Chile, Peru, and Bolivia, in that order. One reason was that it seemed that Spanish would be an easier language to learn. The other reason was that, at the time (1969) it seemed that those countries were the most revolutionary places where Maryknoll was working in South America. Bolivia surprised me, but now, I'm really glad they sent me there, especially because of the rich indigenous culture, which I discovered was so non-Western and truly a "foreign" mission.

I worked in Bolivia for seven years and then pretty much burned out. So I went back to the States to work on promotion, which I did for two years in Minneapolis, my home turf. And then Ron Saucci asked if I wanted to replace him in the Media Relations Office. I jumped at the chance and spent six years at the Knoll, before returning to Bolivia again, where I worked until leaving the Society in 1996.

IC: What types of work were you engaged in?

PN: My golden missionary years were spent in Achacachi, in the Altiplano, among the Aymará indigenous people. It was a wonderful, difficult experience, mainly training native religious leaders, both men and women. They gradually took over much of our pastoral work, especially in their own communities. One Holy Week, we told them to celebrate with their people, like Jesus did at the Last Supper, and remembering his death and resurrection. One catechist reported back that he had gathered the people together on Holy Thursday and acted as Jesus, blessing some soda and bread and sharing these among all the people. Was that a Eucharist???

IC: *Looking back now how do you feel about the work you did? Satisfied? Ambivalent?*

PN: At the time, after several years in the Altiplano, I did not feel too good about it at all. I got tired of coping with the language and culture, though I truly loved the people, especially the catechists. I returned to visit several years later and met Encarnación Huanca, our best woman catechist. She had married a seminarian from the Altiplano, and the bishop gave them a parish to evangelize way, way out in the mountains. She said they repeated the same methods we had done in Achacachi, which said to me that maybe our work resonated with the local culture. She also said, "My parents raised me, but you people made me a woman." I credit that to the Sisters working with us. But it was really something for an Aymará woman to say. Maybe we fit in some way into their ancient, complex, mysterious culture.

Appendix 1   175

IC: *You also had some stateside assignments. Tell us about those.*

PN: I liked Promotion. It gave me a chance to share with people in the States the incredible experiences I had in Bolivia. That expanded in the Media Relations Office. We made films about El Salvador, Zimbabwe, the Philippines, China, Korea, Venezuela, the arms race, and other critical issues. Also, it was the time that Roy Bourgeois disappeared in El Salvador, Pinochet and other dictators reigned in Latin America, Liberation Theology got us branded as "communists," and we had to explain Maryknoll's position to the popular media. *Time, The Wall Street Journal, The New York Times,* and others were all banging on our door for interviews. Jim Noonan, the superior general at the time, was splendid in balancing out the role of the Maryknoll missionary.

IC: *When and where did you and Rebeca first meet and what led up to your departure from the Society and the beginning of your new life and family with Rebeca?*

PN: Rebeca and I met in 1990 when I began work in Cristo Rey parish in Cochabamba. Maryknoll had closed all our parishes in the Altiplano. Tom McBride asked if I wanted to work in a remote section of the parish, where Cathy Breen, a lay missionary, and Rebeca, from the Bolivian Missionary Association worked. He suggested I could celebrate Mass and accompany them in evangelizing the area. I moved into the neighborhood with Brother David McKenna. Rebeca and I organized a lively Basic Christian Community, organized processions for Christmas and Holy Week, formed youth groups and the like. The people eventually built their own church, which we inaugurated. After six years, my term was up.

Rebeca and I had grown close in our work together, and I really appreciated the relationship. So I talked to my family, friends, and Maryknoll and decided to make the move. Even my mom accepted it, considering that the Catholic Church was already accepting married Episcopal priests into its ranks and most other denominations had already accepted a married clergy. Rebeca and I talked it over and really felt the Holy Spirit was leading us in that direction, and that we could continue our missionary vocations in a new way together. At least we wanted to try.

IC: *You decided to stay in Cochabamba after resigning from the Society. That must have been a big decision for you.*

PN: We both loved Cochabamba and wanted to continue on in our mission work there in some way. Besides, we had nowhere else to go. Maryknoll wanted me to leave for a year, to avoid scandal. I suppose they were right in some way. One of our leaders said, "I guess you're just weak like we are." We felt the contrary, that God was really happy with married people. And that would be our new witness. Well, we were married in a civil ceremony in Cochabamba in 1996. Encarnación Huanca, her husband, Calixto, and Padre Julio Rojas came down from the Altiplano. Charlie Winkler and Carmen were our sponsors. A number of lay missioners, along with Bill and Carlota Lafferty, and many, many neighbors joined us in the celebration. We danced until two in the morning.

IC: *What did you do in those years in Cochabamba?*

PN: Our biggest challenge after getting married was getting a job to support ourselves. Fortunately, Dudley Conneely ['71] hired me to work with him in Project Concern International. That saved my butt! After a couple of years, Fr. William Wilson, a former Trappist, hired me to work in his orphanage, where both Rebeca, as a social worker, and I worked until almost the time we returned to the States in May 2012.

IC: *And then you made an even bigger decision…and returned with Rebeca and your family to the States. What inspired you to make that move?*

PN: On the one hand, it was my turn to spend some time with my mom, who was a bright and sassy 97 years old, and still living alone. Rebeca also thought it would be a good experience for her and the children, Elias, 10, and Rose, 7, to experience my culture and learn English.

IC: *What's life been like for you in your home state of Minnesota? How are you all adjusting?*

PN: It's been difficult for Rebeca to leave family relations, so many dear friends, her culture, and her language. And for our daughter, Rose, to leave her little friends and her cuddly dog, Manchas. She still longs for him. I returned through a different door than the one I had left through. I guess I had grown accustomed to life in Bolivia, the attitudes of people there, a slower pace of life, less aggressive, more congenial. Also, we were faced with so many immediate needs: to get the kids in school, buy a car, get insurance, an apartment, and a job and help the children learn English. Gracias a Dios for many good friends who still remembered me and stepped forward when we really needed them to guide us around and lead us through the maze. A year later, it is kind of working out. I got a nice temp job as a hospital interpreter for people who don't speak much English. It's still frustrating for Rebeca dealing with the bureaucracy and English and not getting her social work degree recognized.

IC: *Any big plans for the future?*
PN: Just keep our heads above water. We're still just new immigrants here, and struggling to make ends meet. I actually appreciate the experience of feeling some actual solidarity with the poor and marginated in our society. I'm enjoying writing a fictional novel. And Rebeca needs to get her driver's license and find some meaningful work.

Bolivia is still very dear to us and has a hold on our hearts. We haven't ruled out the possibility of returning to live there once again.

■

Appendix 2

Paul David Newpower, age 81, passed away peacefully in the company of family on January 15, 2023, at 9:03 A.M. Preceded in death by parents, Paul and Rose Newpower and brother Donald. Survived by wife Rebeca, son Elias, daughters Rose and Anabel, brother Tom (Betty), sister-in-law Margaret, grandchildren, cousins Mary (Jack) and John Murphy, three nieces and three nephews.

Paul was born April 14, 1941, in St. Paul, MN. After finishing high school in St. Paul, he went to university with his love for stars which is why he pushed to become an astronaut. After realizing that this was not his path he was given the opportunity to become a priest, but due to his longing and love for travel he ended up becoming an ordained Maryknoll missionary in 1969. He was sent to Bolivia where he learned Spanish and later Aymará because he needed to communicate with the rural people of Achacachi. Until his departure in 1977.

He returned to the USA to continue his mission in the state of MN, then he traveled to different countries with the means of communication and seeking justice for their people. Until 1990 when he went back to Bolivia, Cochabamba. Where he inspired the women of Achacachi to have a voice, helped stabilize families and helped the youth to seek and reach their dreams. He also helped build a church and homes. In 1996 he married Rebeca who became his companion while serving the people. They chose to live in simplicity and had three children, returned to the USA in 2012 where he lived happily until he passed away.

This obituary appeared in the *Twin Cities Pioneer Press*, 22 January 2023.

Photo Credits

7. Top: www.youtube.com/watch?v=QB0K8AqO9Ao. Bottom: Wikimedia Commons. 12. Maryknoll Mission Archives / courtesy Fr. Eugene Toland, MM. 14. Wikimedia Commons / Carla Salazar / 2019. 16. Wikimedia Commons / McGhiever / 2020. 17. Maryknoll Mission Archives. 19. Maryknoll Mission Archives. 22. Roy Bourgeois. 25 and 26. Terry Cedar and Ray Voith (voith-usa.com/SemPix/index.html). 34. Wikimedia Commons / David Peña / January 2007. 37. Newpower family. 38. Dudley Conneely, 2010. 40. Maryknoll Mission Archives / Maryknoll Language Institute. 42. Top: Gaceta del Sur. Bottom: wsws.org. 49. Instituto Humanitas Unisinos. 51. Wikipedia / Dutch National Archives / 24 August 1971. 54. *Atlantic* magazine / Penny Lernoux, "Latin America: The Revolutionary Bishops," July 1980. 55. Wikimedia Commons / Steve Willey / May 2007. 57. Catholic News Agency. 60. Google maps. 61. Fr. Joseph Towle, MM. 65. Wikimedia Commons / Mhwater at Dutch Wikipedia / 2002. 70. Wikimedia Commons / W. Alejandro Valdez Valenzuela / 2018. 77. Fr. Joseph Towle, MM. 78. Joseph Picardi. 81. Wikimedia Commons / Cody Hinchliff / 2007. 82–85. Fr. Eugene Toland, MM. 91. Wikimedia Commons / "El Yatiri," oil on canvas by Arturo Borda (1883–1953). 93. Wikimedia Commons / Juan Santa Cruz Pachacuti. 94. Top: Newpower family. Bottom: NASA. Ground-based image: European Southern Observatory (ESO)/Y. Beletsky; Hubble image: NASA, ESA, and R. Sahai (Jet Propulsion Laboratory); Processing: Gladys Kober (NASA/Catholic University of America). 100. Maryknoll Mission Archives. 102. Newpower family. 108. Roy Bourgeois. 112. "Christ Crucified in Nicaragua." José Ignacio Fletes Cruz is a Primitivista artist, whose naif style of image making is associated with a utopian Christian

community founded in the mid 1960s by the Catholic poet-priest Ernesto Cardenal, in the remote Solentiname island chain at the southern end of Lake Nicaragua. 113. Wikimedia Commons / Tenquique503. 115. Maryknoll Mission Archives. 121. teachingforchange.org. 122. Maryknoll Mission Archives and Maryknoll Sisters. 126. Roy Bourgeois. 127. Wikimedia Commons, 30 April 2014. 129. Maryknoll Mission Archives. 134. Wikimedia Commons / Antonisse, Marcel / Anefo-Dutch National Archives, The Hague, 1984. 135. Wikimedia Commons / Junancy B Wan-derley Jr. / 8 July 2016. 138. *Catholic Worker*, December 1978 / Jim Forest. 141. Wikimedia Commons / Tony Hisgett / January 2009. 144. Maryknoll Mission Archives. 145. Fr. Joseph Towle, MM. 146. Maryknoll Mission Archives. 148. Fr. Joseph Towle, MM. 153. Fr. Eugene Toland, MM. 157. Top: Wikiwand.com. Bottom: Maryknoll Mission Archives. 158. Fr. Joseph Towle, MM. 161–169. Newpower family. 170. Wikimedia Commons / https://www.flickr.com/photos/194792615@N03/51869395074/. 171. Wikimedia Commons. 173. Newpower family.

Images in *Pilgrimage* were selected, placed, and captioned by Tom Fenton, who is responsible for any mistakes or omissions in these credits. Tom thanks the family of Paul Newpower, the staff of Maryknoll Mission Archives, Roy Bourgeois, Terry Cedar, Dudley Conneely, Joe Picardi, Gene Toland, Joe Towle, and Ray Voith for help finding and acquiring the images that appear in *Pilgrimage*.

Lithium Rush in Bolivia

A novel of international intrigue in the scramble to exploit Bolivia's rich deposits of "white gold"

PAUL NEWPOWER

Available from Amazon in print and ebook versions.

Made in the USA
Monee, IL
11 May 2023